COMPOSTING

This book is about compost: how to make it, how to use it, and at the same time how to relate what you are doing to the long-term fruitfulness of the soil which still remains the basis on which the health and stability of our civilization depends.

COMPOSTING

The Cheap and Natural Way
to Make Your Garden Grow

by
Dick Kitto

THORSONS PUBLISHERS LIMITED
Wellingborough, Northamptonshire

First published 1978

© DICK KITTO 1978

This book is sold subject to the condition that it shall not, by way of trade or otherwise, be lent, re-sold, hired out, or otherwise circulated without the publisher's prior consent in any form of binding or cover other than that in which it is published and without a similar condition including this condition being imposed on the subsequent purchaser.

ISBN 0 7225 0487 X (hardback)
ISBN 0 7225 0465 9 (paperback)

Photoset by Specialised Offset Services Limited, Liverpool
and printed in Great Britain by
Weatherby Woolnough, Wellingborough, Northamptonshire
on paper made from 100% re-cycled fibre supplied
by P.F. Bingham Ltd., Croydon, Surrey

CONTENTS

INTRODUCTION

Nowadays an increasing number of people are growing vegetables in their gardens and allotments because of the high cost of food, and for the same sort of reason they start making compost because of the high cost of fertilizers. As their gardens begin to flourish they realize that the vegetables from it are not only cheaper but fresher and tastier than those they buy in the shops. So it is with compost: it is not only cheaper than fertilizer from a bag, it is better.

But there is something else as well: in the memorable words of the Thorpe Report on Allotments 'allotment holdings provide a healthy physical recreation for people of all ages and occupations, especially for those living in a crowded urban environment. It affords relaxation from the stresses of modern life and yet is also creative. It involves the use of numerous mental stimuli, powers of observation and planning, appraisals of beauty in form, scent and colour, the love of nature and the mystique of growing things.'

Gardening, nurturing plants that are healthy, providing food, feeding the waste products back to increase the fertility of the soil, participating in this age-old process by which the whole of the living world has grown and continues to survive, satisfies our inborn instinct for creativity in a way that few other activities can do. There is a sense of wholeness and wholesomeness about it that makes us look with awe at the way our present civilization spreads its asphalt and cement remorselessly over the green countryside, and sprays the remainder with poisons and pollutants.

A central step in this natural cycle of operations is the returning of waste organic material to the soil, and the present interest in compost is only a rediscovery of what has been practised since time immemorial.

Like many of the ways in which the human race has attempted to better its lot on this earth, the principles of composting are derived from observation of natural processes. When waste organic matter is left under natural conditions it will begin to decompose as the result of the action of various organisms. These are chiefly microbial but worms, slugs, small animals and birds, also play their part. In theory this decomposition could continue over the years until the organic matter is completely mineralized, but in normal circumstances this never happens though it comes near to it when organic matter under waterlogged conditions turns into peat and peat into lignite or coal.

At an intermediate stage in this process of decomposition the organic matter becomes compost; this stage is very difficult to define chemically or biologically but relatively easy to recognize in practice by the fact that the material becomes dark brown, fibrous, reasonably homogeneous and has a characteristic clean earthy smell. It is at this stage that, mixed with soil already existing, it becomes an ideal medium for the growth of plants.

This process has been going on naturally for millenia, slowly building up the fertility of the soil; it is in fact, together with the breaking down of the original rock into particles under the action of the weather, the process by which all soil is formed and on which all natural vegetation and therefore all life depends. The compost heap is a device by which this natural process is concentrated and speeded up to cater for the extra demands of intensive growing. By confining large quantities of organic matter into a relatively small space under optimum conditions the speed and efficiency of decomposition is increased so that large quantities of compost can be produced in a short time.

The compost heap is thus an artificial phenomenon, nowhere to be found in nature. In this respect it is no different from all the other operations of agriculture and horticulture: they are all interferences in natural processes and in the natural rhythm of growth and decay; they are all attempts by the human race to swing the ecological balance in its favour. All animals are engaged in a similar struggle for survival; the human race is unique in the intelligence and ingenuity it brings to bear on this struggle, in the scale of its activities and more recently in its ruthlessness.

The organic movement has always stood against many of these trends, and others are beginning to have their doubts. Are modern methods of chemical food production the only or the best ones to meet present day demands? And if they are, may they not be building up problems for future generations which they will be unable to solve?

What we as compost gardeners are aiming to do is not to return to wholly natural conditions, which obviously would be those of the forest and the jungle, but to work sufficiently in harmony with natural processes to establish our own place securely within the existing environment.

This book is about compost: how to make it, how to use it, and at the same time how to relate what we are doing to the long-term fruitfulness of the soil which still remains, as it always has been, the basis on which the health and stability of our civilization depends.

I think there is one thing that needs to be emphasized at the very start, and never to be forgotten: making compost is a simple, natural process. It is going on all the time, in the hedgerows, in the ditches, beneath the grassland, in the forests. Whatever the conditions, nature adapts and the process goes on. It goes on in your kitchen compost bucket, in your gardens, in your compost heap. Anyone who has to do with food will know that it is almost impossible to stop the decomposition of living matter, short of freezing it, sterilizing it or dehydrating it.

The cycle of birth, growth, death and decay is one of the most inevitable laws of nature and whatever you do nature will be on your side and will come to your rescue. So do not be put off by the experts who say 'Oh, you should have done this or that'; do not worry if your compost heap will not heat up, or smells funny, or seems to be waterlogged. None of these things is a total disaster and even if you do nothing about them you will still get compost of a sort eventually.

In this book I have tried to cover the whole process fairly thoroughly, and at first glance this may give the impression that it is all very complicated and you must follow instructions exactly. But that is not the case.

What is true is that the more you understand and the more careful you are the better your compost will be and the quicker you will get it. But do not be downhearted if things do not go right the first time. Do not be flustered by complicated instructions and advice. Take it easy; learn by stages; do what seems sensible; work with nature, and nature will work with you.

1
BASIC PRINCIPLES OF COMPOST MAKING

If you are in the habit of reading gardening books you will find that there are several different and often contradictory views on the best way to make compost. For instance Sir Albert Howard, originator of the 'Indore method', upon which so much of modern compost lore and practice is based, and the first person in modern times to apply an analytical and scientific approach to the subject, tells us to make our heap in a shallow pit. This is doubtless because he originated his method in India where the climate is dry and moisture has to be conserved. But if you live on the western foothills of the Pennines you will be told to build on a mound so as to drain off some of the 70 to 80 inches of rainfall that falls each year.

The important thing is the knowledge not only of what to do, but the reasons for doing it, so that you can modify your methods to suit your particular circumstances.

Aerobic and Anaerobic
Basic to this knowledge is the understanding that there are two methods of composting which superficially are very similar to each other, in that they both involve piling organic matter in heaps in order to aid its decomposition. But they are very different in the way they operate, and this unrecognized difference is one of the causes of much failure and disappointment. The first method is the one which is described or implied in almost all books on the subject, in which the decomposition results mainly from the action of bacteria that require oxygen and that flourish within a temperature range 120° to 150°F (48° to 65°C). These bacteria breed and work very fast and, given the right conditions, will produce usable compost in a month. This method is often described as being 'aerobic', meaning it requires a free flow of air (oxygen) and 'thermophilic' meaning it operates at a high temperature. The second method is one where the bacteria do not require oxygen, and do not generate heat. This method is very much slower and normally takes about a year to produce good compost. It is usually

described as being 'anaerobic', meaning that it does not require air or oxygen. The words 'aerobic' and 'anaerobic' are rather cumbersome, but they are so convenient and so widely understood that it is difficult to avoid using them. I shall therefore use them throughout this book: aerobic will refer principally to a compost heap in which aeration plays a major part; it can also refer to the process of decomposition in such a heap, to the bacteria that cause the decomposition and to the resulting compost. 'Anaerobic' refers to a heap where aeration does not occur, and also to the bacteria and processes that operate in this case.

The majority of compost heaps are aimed at the aerobic method, and perhaps achieve it for a short period; but either from the beginning, or after the first few days, change to being anaerobic.

Undoubtedly the aerobic method has many advantages and produces the better compost. On the other hand it is more difficult, and takes a lot more trouble; and there are certainly occasions when the anaerobic is a simpler and perfectly adequate method.

We have then a choice as to which method to use and before trying to make it we need to look carefully at the two alternatives so that we have some facts and understanding on which to base a comparison.

The Aerobic Method

Before considering the detailed requirements of the aerobic compost heap it is as well to describe briefly the operation as a whole. The main workers in this process are the bacteria, literally billions of millions of them, of many thousands of different species. The requirements of the bacteria are very much the same as our own: food, air, moisture, warmth. As soon as they find themselves in conditions that provide these requirements they begin to breed; once started they breed very fast and the population increases dramatically. This creates energy in the form of heat, and the heap starts to warm up; the original species of bacteria find the going too hot and die off, to be replaced by new species, the thermophilic bacteria, which flourish in these higher temperatures. The plant food is consumed, transformed, excreted and recycled. Many different species of bacteria move in as the temperature rises still further.

To us humans this is a familiar scene: it is a growth economy gone mad, a rising population making more and more demands on the limited resources of their little world of the compost heap: there is bound to be a reckoning. The limiting factor, as perhaps in our own society, is the demand for energy. For the energy of the heap, which manifests itself as heat, comes from the combination of the carbon in the plant materials and the oxygen in the air that fills the pore spaces: slowly but inevitably the oxygen is used up in the process, to be replaced by carbon dioxide and the spectre of suffocation looms ahead; unmindful, the bacteria continue their breeding; but it is no good: the end is near. The pore spaces are clogged, the great food reserves of carbon lie untouched by the oxygen-starved bacteria, the temperature falls; the cycle is complete.

Now there advances upon this scene of desolation the bacterial vultures – the anaerobic bacteria. The lack of oxygen does not worry them, it is to their advantage for now they have the field to themselves; they can take their time as they methodically colonize this little universe and prepare for the long year's haul ahead.

The rise and fall of this compost civilization will have taken less than a week and its progress can be measured by anyone with a silage thermometer, for it runs parallel with the rise and fall of the temperature. If this is plotted on a graph, it will look something like this:

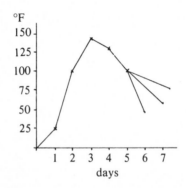

The speed of decline of temperature after day 5 will depend on the insulation properties of the heap, but one can expect that it will fall in a gradual curve and after about three weeks the heap will have reverted to roughly the temperature of the surrounding soil.

This, then, is a picture of how a well-made heap, initially aerobic, will very rapidly become anaerobic – an inevitable process unless steps are taken to counteract it. The key factor is obvious: it is the shortage of oxygen. And so if you wish to maintain a rapid, high-temperature, aerobic heap, you must allow the suffocating carbon dioxide to escape, open out the pore spaces and replenish them once more with life-giving oxygen. The most straightforward way of doing this is to turn the heap, and as soon as you do this the whole life cycle begins again.

If you study this cycle it is clear what environmental conditions you should aim at:

Food

This is the composition of the materials that go to make the heap. There must be a variety of this to sustain life. Bacteria do not live on carbon and oxygen alone but require a wide variety of nutrients just as other animals do. A shortage of carbon is not in normal circumstances likely to be a limiting factor, except perhaps in the case of a pile entirely composed of soft, sappy, green material (e.g. lawn mowings). Apart from oxygen, the commonest shortage is of nitrogen, another essential ingredient of living things (the whole question of nitrogen content will receive special attention in the next section).

Moisture

There must be as much moisture as possible, but never so much that the pore spaces become waterlogged. In other words, the compost heap must be damp but not wet.

Heat

The heap must be enabled to heap up, and this involves some form of insulation.

Air

Providing these first three conditions are correct, the limiting factor is aeration, and to maintain this is the major requirement for aerobic decomposition.

We will now turn to these four requirements and consider them in turn in a little more detail.

Composition of Materials

Anything that has lived will make compost, but some things are better than others. For example, pine needles are unsuitable because they contain a resin that is detrimental to the growth of most plants. Dead pigs are unsuitable because they are illegal – a few years ago a farmer was prosecuted for having a dead pig in his manure heap. Most people know that if you make a heap entirely of grass mowings it will produce nothing but a slimy black mass. If you make a heap entirely of broccoli stalks the end product will still be broccoli stalks. What is needed is a mixture, but even then some care is needed in selecting the ingredients.

The principal criterion for this selection is the proportion of carbon and nitrogen in the materials. Both these elements are essential to the life of bacteria, and the proportion between them is a critical factor. All animal and vegetable matter contain both of them in varying concentrations. In general, carbon is

CARBON-NITROGEN RATIO IN COMPOST			
	N	*C*	*Remarks*
Urine	XXXX		Potash
Dried Blood	XXXX		
Fish Waste	XXX		Phosphates
Poultry Manure	XXX		Phosphates; very 'hot'
Cow Manure	XXX		Without straw
Lawn Mowings	XX		
Comfrey	XX		Potash
Pomace	XX		
Hops	XX		
Tomato Haulms	XX	X	
Pig Manure	XX		Cold
Farmyard Manure	XXX	XX	Including straw as usually found (fresh)
Seaweed	XX	X	Potash (varies a little)
Legume Tops	XX		
Legume Whole	XX	X	
Peas and Bean Haulms	XX		
Horse Manure	XX	X	Including straw
Fern	X	X	Potash, if cut green
Peat	X	X	
Oat Straw	X	XX	
General Garden Weeds	X	XX	
Newspaper		XX	
Wheat Straw		XXX	
Woody Stems, Hard Brassica Stalks		XXX	
Sawdust		XXXX	

present in woody matter, hard stalks and roots; nitrogen is concentrated in the leaf and green part of the plant, and also in the little white nodules to be found on the roots of leguminous plants – peas, beans, clovers and vetches.

The amounts of carbon and nitrogen in the original organic matter should be roughly in the proportion of 30:1, which during the process of decomposition will reduce to about 10:1. This reduction comes about because, as already explained, a proportion of the carbon combines with oxygen to produce energy in the form of heat and is released as carbon dioxide waste, in exactly the same way as we consume carbohydrates and oxygen and breathe out carbon dioxide. If there is too much carbon, decomposition will be slowed down and the correct temperature will not be reached. If there is too much nitrogen this will be lost and wasted. As the ratio 30:1 is rather meaningless to most people I have prepared the accompanying table as a guide.

In selecting materials you should attempt to maintain a balance between the number of carbon crosses and the number of nitrogen crosses. For instance, if you have a lot of wheat straw (XXX carbon) you should try to balance it with an equal quantity of, say, poultry droppings (XXX nitrogen) or a larger quantity of comfrey (XX nitrogen), and so on. This table, by the way, shows why the combination of cow dung and straw is such a satisfactory one, as they balance each other with high proportions of carbon and nitrogen. However, in farm heaps there is often a tendency for the proportion of dung to be too great, with a consequent loss of nitrogen in the form of ammonia, which accounts for the pungent smell given off in the early stages.

Luckily for us nature is very accommodating and is determined to make things grow (think of the 1,000,000,000 spermatozoa to produce one baby!) so there is no need to keep to these quantities accurately; they are a guide only, but the nearer you keep to them the better compost you will make.

Another important factor is size of material: obviously the bacteria mainly attack the surface of the material so that large pieces with a low ratio of surface to volume are slow to decompose. In addition the surface often consists of a hard protective layer which acts as a barrier to the more easily decomposed matter beneath. It is therefore important that large pieces of material should be chopped up as small as possible – the surface of a brassica stalk is roughly trebled if it is chopped into pieces one inch long.

A third factor is the chemical quality of the carbon compounds, for some of these are far more resistant to decay than others. Even in the form of sawdust, many woods will take well over two years to decay into compost, and will require a large supply of nitrogen to do so. It is important to be very cautious about incorporating such materials into a compost heap that you expect to use within this time. The employment of sawdust as a surface mulch is a controversial subject which will be discussed later.

Aeration

As already explained, the life-style of microbes is self-destructive because in using up the available oxygen they release in its place carbon dioxide which fills the pore places previously occupied by air. In other words they suffocate themselves by over-breeding in a limited environment. This can happen very rapidly. A heap will usually rise to maximum activity and begin to decline again within five days.

Much of the technology of large-scale composting is directed towards aeration, usually by means of some form of continuous agitation or turning and mixing, and this emphasizes the key importance of this operation. There is no doubt that *continuous* turning provides the quickest and most efficient way of making good compost and that the nearer you approach this ideal the better things will be. Unfortunately there is no substitute for turning, and most of the other suggestions proposed for improving aeration are more or less useless, if not actually detrimental. However I think it worth while to take a look at a few of these suggestions, if only to save people labour and disappointment.

Some people advocate putting lines of bricks along the bottom of the heap to create air channels. Others propose building the heap on a wire mesh. These proposals, with appropriate diagrams, work well in books, but are not entirely trouble-free when it comes to actually making the heap.

How, for instance, are you actually going to get the compost out at the end? The normal and undoubtedly the best way to shovel anything is to slide your spade or shovel along at floor level – and how can you do this if you go slap bang into a line of bricks or get entangled in a mesh of wire netting?

But there is another factor; these methods are ineffective because, as the bacteria gnaw and nibble away at the organic matter, masticate it, metabolize it, digest it, excrete it, they diminish its bulk (just as we do when we eat lettuces and endives and chicory and excrete little brown compact sausages) and this causes the whole mass of the compost heap to compact down, forming an airtight mass which no amount of wire mesh can aerate.

Much the same comments are applicable to plunging iron pipes in from the top to form air vents: experience has shown that even pipes pumping forced air through vents have not been very successful because the air penetrates so unevenly.

Another method advocated is to make the sides of the bin slatted, so that air can penetrate inwards through the heap. Again, it is extremely doubtful whether this will succeed in its object, but even if it does to a small extent you are coming up against the problem of insulation, because the purpose of the container is principally to insulate the heap, and if you leave gaps in it this will obviously cut down its insulating properties. In addition, the flow of air through the slats will cause the surface of the heap to dry out at these points and almost no decomposition will take place.

In fact the demand for aeration is incompatible with the demand for insulation, and although it is the need for aeration that is the most important of these by this method you are getting very little of the former at a considerable loss of the latter.

The experience of nearly all compost makers has demonstrated that, if you wish to maintain your compost heap in an aerated condition, the only sure method is to turn it as frequently as possible. How frequently you turn is rather up to you, and will be discussed further under the mixed aerobic/anaerobic section; but if you want to obtain the *maximum* aerobic efficiency you should aim to turn your heap every three or four days, in which case, other things being well, you should produce compost in about twelve days, that is with three turns. But do not worry; it is not in the least *essential* to turn your heap this often; I am only stating the way to get the very best results – a doctrine of perfection that very few people manage to achieve.

Moisture

The amount of moisture present is very important, for bacteria cannot flourish in dry conditions. Equally, aerobic bacteria will be drowned in over-wet conditions, though of course anaerobic decomposition will occur even in a completely waterlogged state: that, as already mentioned, is how peat is formed, but the process takes several thousands of years. The difference in rainfall between the east and the west of England, and to a lesser extent between winter and summer, is sufficient to affect the process profoundly, and must be taken into account when making the heap. The only reliable way of controlling the amount of moisture present is to protect the heap from variations in weather conditions, and provide the water artificially.

This, then, is one good reason for containing the heap in a box and putting a roof on it. It is also a good reason against starting it off in a pit, unless you are building it on a soil that is very porous indeed.

In fact, protecting it against waterlogging from below is almost as important as protecting it against flooding from above. If your soil is at all heavy it is worth building the heap in a slightly raised position and leaving gaps at the bottom of the walls to ensure that it keeps well drained and dried out at the bottom (note that these gaps are nothing to do with aeration).

Temperature

The artificiality of an aerobic compost heap is most noticeably manifested in the temperature it reaches. Natural decomposition rarely results in a rise in temperature beyond a very few degrees, so that throughout the duration of the process roughly consistent conditions prevail and roughly the same micro-organisms will operate. In an aerobic compost heap, on the other hand, the rapid increase in temperature gives rise to quite a different class of organism (the thermophilic bacteria) and it is interesting to speculate on the fact that these organisms, absent under natural conditions, nevertheless occur spontaneously when the conditions that suit them arise. Where do they come from? Where have they been lurking, all these thousands of millions of years, as it were waiting in ambush for man to invent the first compost heap?

These organisms, whose occurrence is so intriguing and inexplicable, represent a lucky break for gardeners, for they enable the good composter to achieve two important results: the destruction of weed seeds and perennial roots; and the destruction of pathogenic bacteria. Both of these certainly occur with a temperature of 150°F (65°C) but also happen almost as effectively with a damp temperature of 120°F (49°C) lasting over a period of several days.

A temperature of somewhere between 120° and 150°F (49°-65°C) represents a goal for composters which is hard to achieve. For, whereas the other factors mentioned – composition, aeration and moisture – are largely under our control, temperature is not. The correct temperature occurs naturally when the other conditions are right, or at least it should do so. Sometimes, inexplicably, it does not and then the composter is stumped, because if the temperature has not risen, then the bacteria are not breeding, and that means the compost is not working and there is very little he can do but start again.

Insulation

The principal way in which we can improve the situation is by ensuring that the heap is insulated. In a very large heap the outside layers act as an insulation barrier for the inner layers; but there is a minimum size below which the heat losses from the surface are so great that the heap will never heat up sufficiently, however well made it is in other respects and however much activity the bacteria engender. This size is in the region of 10 by 8 by 5 ft (3 by 2.5 by 1.5m) high and so is beyond the reach of the ordinary small gardener or allotment holder.

For smaller heaps some sort of insulation has to be provided, normally in the form of a bin or box. Here again there is still a minimum size below which even a boxed-in heap will not retain enough heat, and this is usually taken to be a 3 or 4 foot (1 or 1.25m) cube, though this depends very much on the climate. The heat losses on an exposed part of the north west of Scotland are very different from those in a south-facing garden in Torquay.

The Question of Size

This question of size poses one of the major and largely unacknowledged problems for the small gardener. For the reality of his situation is that his main compost ingredients, kitchen refuse and garden waste, come in small quantities every day or so, and so it is only after a considerable period that its quantity builds up to enough to make a reasonable sized heap. What he tends to do is to put material on the heap as it comes so that in its vital early stages of decomposition it never attains the critical size to enable the temperature to build up. Thus the initial phases of bacterial activity which should have been raising the temperature to thermophilic conditions is largely wasted.

One solution to this is to form a co-operative composting arrangement with neighbours, so that at one weekened, say, enough material can be gathered together to fill one member's heap to the top, and the next weekend the next person's heap is filled and so on. I have heard of arrangements like this but have never actually come across one in practice.

The other method does not involve neighbours and will be described in chapter 2.

The Anaerobic Method

This is the method that is familiar, for instance, in heaped turf, where inverted turves are stacked and left for about twelve months to become 'turf loam', a basic ingredient of John Innes Potting Compost. It is also familiar in many compost heaps that have not maintained their initial aeration. This method will not destroy perennials, so it is important to exclude these. In theory it is possible to chop them up, hammer and crush them and lay them out in the sun to wither and die; but it is much safer to put them on the 'rough heap' (see page 45) or burn them and use the ash. Nor will it kill weed seeds or pathogenic bacteria, so anything liable to go putrid should be excluded — animal or fish wastes, for example. Manure may be used provided it is covered up, though, as will be explained later, it is wasteful to use fresh manure in an anaerobic heap when it could be used as an activator for an aerobic one.

Apart from this the anaerobic heap has few limitations and restrictions. Naturally bacterial activity will slow down during cold weather and in fact will more or less come to a halt during a hard winter, so even here there is an advantage in 'boxing in' the heap. In any case it is advisable to cover the heap so that it does not cause a nuisance. Again, the degree of moisture is not nearly so critical. The main danger is that uncovered heaps get very wet and cold during the winter, when they will putrify rather than decompose.

That is about all there is to it. The process will take about a year, and the end product may well have quite a lot of rough material mixed in it. It is liable also to be rather sticky, and may be too acid. The best procedure is to fork it over, remove the rough material to pass on to the next heap, loosen and aerate what is left, apply lime, and leave it to mature in the open for about a month before using.

Generally speaking the anaerobic heap has received a very rough deal from composters, but it has many advantages: in particular it is useful for the production of turf loam, which, quite apart from its use in John Innes compost, is a valuable form of composted soil: for rough heaps, for large quantities of rough grass, straw and the like, and for material that has a lot of soil in it. Before attempting to make any final choice between the two methods it is worth listing their comparative advantages and disadvantages.

Aerobic	*Anaerobic*
Requires quite careful preparation and continued attention	Requires very little preparation or attention
Can include almost any organic material	Must not include perennial weeds or hard materials
Normally requires boxing in or containing	Does not need boxing or containing
Must be of a minimum size	Can be any size
Requires turning	Does not require turning
Produces compost in one to two months (depending on the season)	Takes about a year to produce compost
Will kill all weed-seeds, and most perennial roots	Does not kill weed-seeds or perennial roots
Kills all pathogenic bacteria, does not produce odours or flies or other vermin	May produce odours, and flies, so should be carefully covered over
Produces a compost that is fairly homogeneous and of about the right degree of acidity and ready for immediate use	May produce a rather cold, heavy compost, rather too acid, with some uncomposted fragments, which will require sieving before use
Does not require liming	Probably requires liming
Requires careful attention to carbon/nitrogen ratio, i.e. is likely to require an activator	Does not require attention to carbon/nitrogen ratio

The Mixed Heap

There is no reason why these two methods should not be combined and this is probably the best choice for the person who has limited time at his disposal. Let us look at how most people operate their compost heaps.

As materials come to hand they are deposited in the compost bin over a period of a couple of months or so. This happens very unevenly. After a weekend of gardening there are a lot of weeds; once a week or perhaps once a month the chicken shed is cleaned out and there's a layer of straw and manure; or there may be a party and a whole lot of kitchen waste appears. But in any case, for most of the time, the size of this heap will be below the critical size for proper thermophilic decomposition.

If the mixture is about right aerobic activity will start, but the temperature will never build up because of the surface losses, the oxygen will be used up, and anaerobic decomposition will set in. If the building of the heap is spread over not too long a period there will certainly be some rise in temperature before it settles into a gradual anaerobic decline. What has prevented the proper initial build-up of aerobic activity has been the fact that this was dissipated gradually over too long a period.

If at this stage, that is when a complete binful of material has accumulated, the heap is turned then a fair amount of aerobic activity will follow and a fair heat will be achieved before it reverts to its anaerobic state. Failure results partly because people mistakenly expect a heap to remain heated and active over a long period without attention, which is both theoretically and practically impossible, and partly because the slow build-up of the heap in the early stages allows too much of the initial energy to be dissipated. Of course there are other possible reasons for failure connected with the ingredients and other factors, but assuming that these are more or less correct there are three choices open to the compost makers:

To eliminate all perennial weeds, animal and other obnoxious materials, and burn them on the bonfire, and opt for a trouble-free anaerobic heap with a through-put of about twelve months.

To aim for an aerobic heap and be prepared for turning at least once a week and preferably twice a week, with a through-put of a month or less.

To settle for a mixed process, which is a combination of these two, and is really a rationalization of what most people actually do, or attempt to do. In this, the early stages whilst the quantity of material is being built up until there is enough to make a minimum-sized heap, is anaerobic. The heap is then built, decomposes aerobically, is possibly turned after a week or so, and then allowed to revert to anaerobic conditions, in which it remains until ready. This process would take two to three months during the summer and rather longer during winter.

It seems to me that this method is the one best suited to most gardeners' needs, and it is the one I shall describe in the next two chapters.

2
PRACTICAL COMPOSTING

Since there is much to be said for erecting a sturdy bin that is more or less permanent, it is necessary to choose a site that is also permanent. However, it is best to try out the site for a season to make sure it is the best one before committing yourself.

It is hard to be dogmatic about size, because that depends on how devoted a composter you are and what method you use. But as a rough guide you need an area six times the size of your compost bin. This assumes that you will have a double bin, as explained below, so that if you aim for a bin 4 feet square (1.25m) you will actually erect two bins adjacent to each other, making an area 8 by 4 ft (2.5 by 1.25m) and a total site area of 10 ft (3m) square. This is the *minimum* and will be quite a squeeze, so if you can spare it, a larger area would be better. For a garden the size of a standard allotment (90 by 30 ft, 27 by 9m) a minimum of 12 ft ($3\frac{1}{2}$m) square would be needed, though for this size of garden considerably larger compost bins would be advisable.

It should also be borne in mind that the site should be:

easily accessible by paths

reasonably near a water supply

close to the kitchen – but not too close!

shielded from view

reasonably level

protected from sunshine and the prevailing wind – this can be accomplished by using an area under shady trees which is not otherwise used as a growing area

have good drainage (it is preferable for the heap to rest on earth, though a concrete base is acceptable if it slopes slightly to provide drainage.)

The Compost Bin

On this site you erect a double bin (see illustration). As pointed out above, it is as well in the first instance to make it either a temporary or a portable structure until you have made quite sure that the site you selected is really right.

Having examined quite a number of garden compost heaps it is obvious that most people take far less trouble and care with this operation than it demands. Composting is the cornerstone of organic gardening and even in a small garden the heap may produce many hundredweights of valuable material a year, yet often the most well-organized gardeners seem to slip into slip-shod methods when it comes to composting. Even in financial terms a few pounds laid out at the start will soon garner a rich harvest of profit.

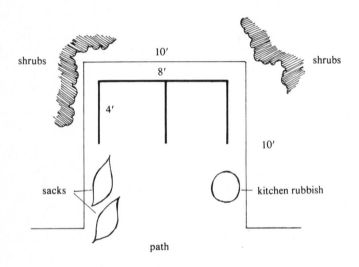

SITING OF HEAP

Constructing the Bin

The material for making the bin must be strong, retain its shape, be weatherproof and reasonably long-lasting. On all these counts wood, though expensive and getting more so every day, is ideal. On the other hand, one of the best heaps I have ever seen was in the angle between two sides of a brick-walled garden, the other two sides being corrugated iron.

I do not recommend wire netting or empire fencing stuffed or lined with newspaper. In principle this is a cheap and simple method, but in practice the wire gets out of shape and looks very unsightly if one is not careful. It is also difficult to fix on a stable roof.

It is worth keeping an eye on local demolition sites or consulting the classified advertisements in the local paper for suitable second-hand wood. So long as the uprights are sound I see no reason why one should not use planking that has been discarded because of woodworm and replace it as it breaks up. Ideally the corner uprights should be at least 5 feet (1.5m) long, preferably of 4 by 2 in (10 by 5cm), and the planks one inch (2.5cm) thick.

The following diagrams show the basic method of construction:

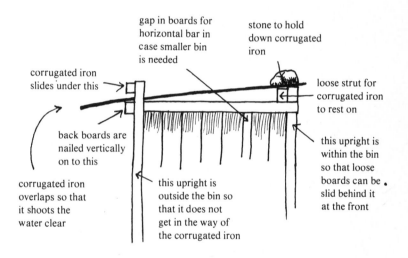

gap in boards for horizontal bar in case smaller bin is needed

stone to hold down corrugated iron

corrugated iron slides under this

loose strut for corrugated iron to rest on

back boards are nailed vertically on to this

this upright is within the bin so that loose boards can be slid behind it at the front

corrugated iron overlaps so that it shoots the water clear

this upright is outside the bin so that it does not get in the way of the corrugated iron

SIDE VIEW OF COMPOST BIN

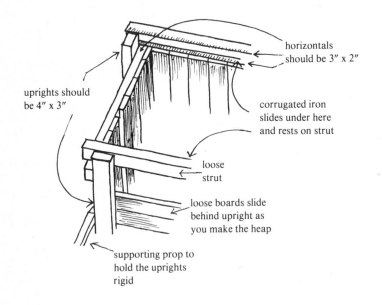

uprights should
be 4″ x 3″

horizontals
should be 3″ x 2″

corrugated iron
slides under here
and rests on strut

loose
strut

loose boards slide
behind upright as
you make the heap

supporting prop to
hold the uprights
rigid

VIEW OF COMPOST BIN FROM THE TOP

For a really first-class job (once you have decided on a permanent site) you could concrete the corner posts into the ground; otherwise hammer them into the ground to a depth of at least 15 in (40cm). It is important that they should be creosoted or tarred where they will be underground, but otherwise left plain.

The fourth (removable) side often presents carpentry problems because the uprights are insufficiently stable and splay apart allowing the loose planks to fall out. It is therefore necessary to keep the uprights rigid, either by a loose strut which holds the side planks together, or by a strong angled support (as shown).

Provided the heap is not too small and is not too exposed to sun, rain and prevailing winds, the fourth side can be left open, though it is preferable to close it, since, apart from anything else, this enables you to get more in your heap.

Two boxes should normally be built together in the form of an E, with each bin the same size. The bins must be covered, or coverable, most simply by corrugated iron which slides through the gap in the back and is held in place in the front by heavy weights. The roof slopes towards the back end so as to discharge water away from the heap and it is as well to have the ground sloping away from the heap where the water discharges so that water does not run back into it. For this reason it is advisable to have the corrugated iron long enough for there to be about a 12 in (30cm) overhang at the back.

A possible alternative is an old carpet, (which, as it disintegrates, can later be incorporated into the heap) which you rest on the top of the heap when it is finished. This has the advantage of being a good insulator, but it is not very good at getting rid of the water and it is really better to use this as well as the corrugated iron roof rather than instead of it.

Ingredients

Now, what are we to use to fill our boxes? First of all, of course, materials from our own gardens and kitchens, and, possibly if we can get it, those of our friends and neighbours. Secondly, it is astonishing how much organic matter it is possible to lay your hands on if you really try, even if you live in an urban area. The first thing to do is to provide yourself with a number of plastic bags. The one hundredweight fertilizer bag is very common and a useful size. In fact these bags litter the countryside and are becoming a serious disposal problem and anyone who has some will probably be willing to give you a few, for instance a local farmer, garden centre, greengrocer, provision merchant, etc. Electricity showrooms often have very large ones in which stoves are wrapped. However, if you cannot get hold of these it is possible to obtain waste disposal bags quite cheaply at your local store. If you then present these to your local grocer or greengrocer, there is a very good chance that he will allow you to fill them with his refuse.

If you go to the seaside take a bag and collect seaweed; to the moors, peat. Ask your local brewery for hops or must; your local cidermaker for pomace; your local woollen mill for shoddy; your local maltster for kiln dust; your local seed merchant for spoiled seeds. Keep your eyes open for hessian sacks rotting in backyards, rotting leaves in ditches, wood ash from bonfires, lawn mowings dumped in the corner of the local park. Talk to the local parks superintendent and the road gangs. In the autumn collect leaves, in the summer grass mowings.

Every day huge quantities of organic matter, the precious end-product of millions of years of evolution, are wastefully disposed of in both town and country, and any keen and watchful enthusiast can reap the benefit. Do not worry if, to start with, you feel rather self-conscious and eccentric; people will not despise you for this activity, they will respect you; in due course your reputation will spread and small boys will travel miles to bring you a bag of horse-droppings or a couple of old birds-nests. Not only will you be collecting compost-material, you will be enriching your whole life, and other people's too.

shake
up and
down

Whatever you collect, keep it well sealed and tidy in its plastic bag until you are ready for it. Each time you have finished adding to the bag shake it down and tie it tightly with string, or fold the top over and hold it down firm with a stone. Empty your kitchen waste into one of those large plastic dustbins with a lid. If it is very wet, as it often may be, mix some dry material with it, and cover it over with a piece of plastic pressed down tight, as well as putting on the lid. If you do not have a spare dustbin, kitchen refuse can also be kept in a plastic bag, but press it down tightly so that no air can get in.

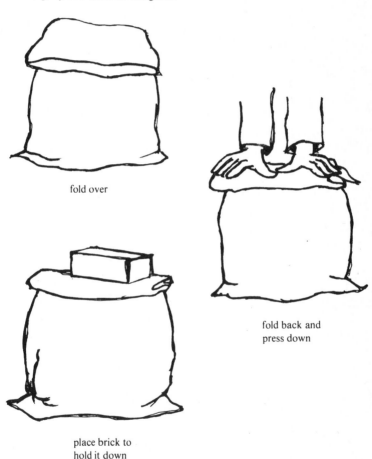

fold over

fold back and
press down

place brick to
hold it down

By now you will probably have tuned in to what we are doing. We are collecting all the ingredients for our compost heap, putting them in bags to seal them off so that no air can get to them and they cannot start decomposing aerobically, so that in due course when we have enough material gathered to make the heap in one fell swoop the material will be more or less fresh and not partially composted already. It is possible to keep organic matter in its original state for a considerable time so long as you exclude air. For instance apple must, the residue of cider-making which is one of the most rapid and efficient compost ingredients there is will remain almost completely unchanged for at least twelve months. Even in the open, a large heap will form a strong dark impervious crust on the outside but will remain unchanged underneath. Once stirred or disturbed to allow the oxygen in, the heap will warm up and begin to decompose and turn dark within a couple of days. Similarly, hops will remain more or less unchanged for several months in a sealed bag. The only change that may take place is for it to become a little more compressed, damp and sticky. When you use it you must shake it and fluff it a bit with your fork.

compost material in dustbin, plastic cover held down by bricks to keep it airtight

Garden Rubbish

Meanwhile we are collecting our garden rubbish in the first of the two compost bins. When you do this lay all the stalks and stems lengthwise, that is from front to back. Shake as much earth off the roots as possible, for although a compost heap benefits from some earth there is generally speaking too much of this so you should avoid adding any extra. Once again you should press all this material down and if possible cover it with a plastic or other sheet to discourage bacterial activity.

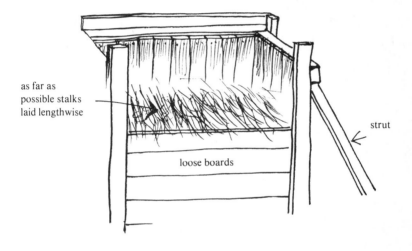

as far as
possible stalks
laid lengthwise

strut

loose boards

FILLING THE FIRST BIN

This process continues until you estimate that you have enough material to fill the second bin.

Building the Aerobic Heap

And now at last comes the day when you are ready to start your aerobic heap. The essential implement for this is a fairly heavy spade with its end sharpened on a carborundum stone or grindstone to razor sharpness. This is used on a guillotine principle to slice off the outer end of the garden heap (the garden refuse in the first bin) into inch sections. You can do this quite rapidly, like a French chef chopping up leeks, so long as there is not too much rough tough grass in it. That is why the stalks and other hard materials were laid as nearly lengthwise as possible – by this process the whole of your garden material is chopped up into the sort of size that will decompose readily.

When you have cut a fair-sized pile you add suitable proportions of materials from your various plastic bags. Mix these together quite roughly with your fork and try to judge whether the mixture is too wet, too dry or just right. It should be damp enough to glisten without being actually wet. If it is too dry you must water it, and do not skimp with the water. It is no good sprinkling water on it with a fine rose. It takes twelve gallons of water to dampen a bale of straw. On the other hand do not forget that most green material is eighty or ninety per cent water and that this will be released when it decomposes. If you have a lot of dry material it is probably best to leave it out for a few days in the rain before you use it. If the material is too wet, you must add some dry matter.

Now, toss it with a fork as lightly as possible into the second bin, and return to your slicing. Repeat this process until you have used up all the material, cover it with sacks or an old carpet or earthy weeds, anything to keep the heat in; put on the corrugated iron roof, and the job is done.

Dry Materials

I said above, mix in dry materials, and it is worth looking at what suitable materials there may be available.

Bonfire ash should be gathered dry and stacked away in sacks.

Wool shoddy, if you can get it, is wonderfully water-absorbent, though it has to be broken up and fluffed out before using it.

Remains of old potting compost etc, should be dried out and bagged up for such an occasion as this.

Peat is of course the ideal material if you can afford it – that is, the light-coloured very dry sphagnum peats like Irish Shamrock peat, not the dark sedge peat from Somerset, which normally has a very high water content itself.

Do not use newspaper; it will go soggy.

You can use sawdust in very small quantities, but it decomposes slowly and too much will certainly hold the heap back. In fact apart from this special use I don't generally recommend using sawdust in the compost heap.

chop downwards

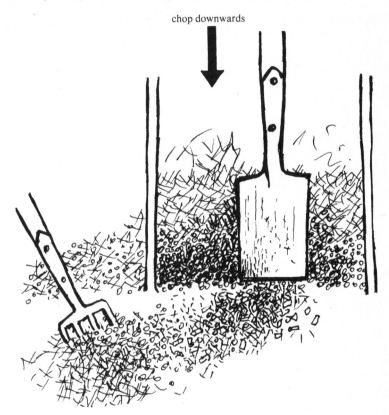

BREAK UP AND FORK INTO NEW HEAP ALONGSIDE

What to Avoid
What to avoid? Very little, except that this is the stage when you should consult the list on page 14 showing proportions of carbon and nitrogen, and this is the second most common cause of heaps that will not heat up and decompose. If you have not got the proportions approximately right your

heap will not heat up, and you will need to take a plastic bag and a shovel to Trafalgar Square (pigeon droppings have one of the highest nitrogen contents of any manure) or attend a few meetings of the local hunt or visit your local garden centre with a Credit Card in your pocket. The shortage of nitrogen is one of the key limiting factors in compost-making and is referred to again later in this chapter under 'activators'.

What else to avoid? Well, how confident are you, from experience, of creating a heap that will heat up to around 150°F (65°C)? And how willing are you to turn your heap at least once so that the outside edges which did not heat up are turned to the inside? If the answer to either of these questions is 'no' then you should avoid putting in the more malevolent perennials. Do not worry so much about docks and dandelions and the like, they can be recovered fairly easily and it is worth trying to compost them down by feeding them through several cycles. It is the more insidious and pervasive weeds, ground elder, convolvulus, celandine, which have very little to contribute to the compost heap or the soil and for which there seems no alternative to a total, if undeserved, annihilation on the bonfire.

I think, too, that in these circumstances you would do well to avoid too many hard or woody materials such as brassica stalks, raspberry canes or hedge clippings.

The Next Stage

So now your heap is made and it lies enigmatically smouldering beneath its canopy of carpets and corrugated iron. What is going on within its mysterious depths? Nervously you regard it and try to uncover its secrets. What imperial splendour, what heights of thermophilic ecstacy are being scaled, what depths of bacterial squalor are being plumbed?

So far there is no Gibbon to trace the intricate webs of this history, for even the scientists are baffled by the incredible variety and complexity of it. But you do have a rough yardstick of whether all is well, and that is the temperature. You do not need a thermometer for this but a simple iron pipe 2 or 3 feet (1 metre) long. You push this in towards the centre of the heap, leave it for a couple of minutes and then withdraw it. If it is too hot to hold comfortably by its business end, then your temperature is above the 120°F (49°C) range and all is going well. After about four days you will probably notice that the pipe is coming out a bit less hot and you will know that your heap is beginning to turn anaerobic and the slow decline has begun.

Turning the Heap

Now you have a choice before you: to turn or not to turn? The situation of your heap at this stage is this. The centre of it will be pretty well free of weed seeds and of all but the largest and most resistant perennial roots; that is to say, these things will still be there, *partially* decomposed perhaps, but no longer capable of germination. It will be no means decomposed, but a start will have been made. The outside of the heap, however, will have changed very little and will be full of weeds and weed seeds. If left now it will probably take another two to three months (in the summer) before the centre is well broken down. At that stage you can chop off the outer 6 in (15cm) all the way round and transfer them to the next heap; the rest can be forked out, removing any large lumps together with any assorted, uncompostable objects that always seem to find their way in via the kitchen wastes such as milk bottle tops, toothpaste tubes and plastic bags. It should then be used as soon as possible.

Alternatively, you can improve both the speed of action and the quality of the end product by turning. Use precisely the same method as in making the heap: that is, guillotine it down with a sharpened spade, fork it in, checking the moisture content as you go and applying the same remedies if it is too wet or too dry. The front 6 in (15cm) should be chopped off first and placed in the centre of the new bin, and the top should also be lifted off and broken up separately and placed in the middle. As this operation is taking place only a week or so after the initial making of the heap, you will not have collected very much material for your next heap and this will have to be shifted out of the way.

It may seem that all this talk about insulation and maintaining the temperature is irrelevant, since the turning process must cool it down almost to nothing. This is true, but as a matter of experience the fact is that the enormous boost the heap receives from its renewed supply of oxygen will bring the temperature right up again within two or three hours after turning.

This turning will both improve the end-product, making it more homogeneous and more weed-free, and speed the process up so that you may well get compost within four to five weeks during the summer months.

Of course, if you wish, after about another week, as the temperature begins to drop once more, you can turn it again, in which case you would be approaching the situation of a fully aerobic heap. In fact the main difference between the fully aerobic and the mixed heap is in the frequency with which you turn it and the care with which you ensure that its outside edges are turned into the centre to make sure that your end product is weed-free and sterilized. However, if you do turn it a third time you will have some problem with double use of bins, and it may be advisable for you to have a triple bin.

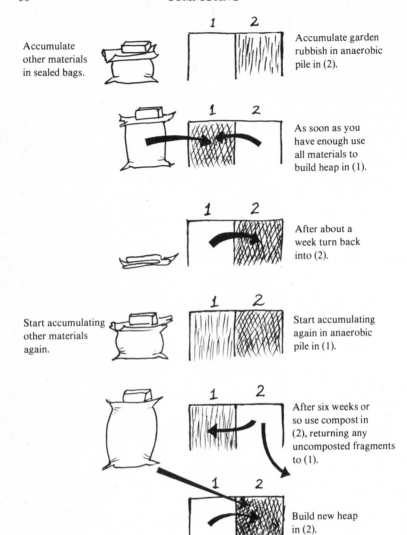

Accumulate other materials in sealed bags.

Accumulate garden rubbish in anaerobic pile in (2).

As soon as you have enough use all materials to build heap in (1).

After about a week turn back into (2).

Start accumulating other materials again.

Start accumulating again in anaerobic pile in (1).

After six weeks or so use compost in (2), returning any uncomposted fragments to (1).

Build new heap in (2).

and so on.

SCHEME FOR MIXED AEROBIC/ANAEROBIC HEAP, WITH ONE TURNING, GIVING COMPOST IN APPROXIMATELY TWO MONTHS (DURING SUMMER MONTHS)

Scheme for fully aerobic heap with three turns at intervals of five days, giving finished compost in roughly three weeks. The third bin is used solely for accumulation of garden rubbish in an anaerobic heap, preparatory to making the heap proper. It could therefore be open, covered merely with a plastic sheet, rather than a third bin. By this method you should produce at least 15 tons of compost a year, worth well over £200.

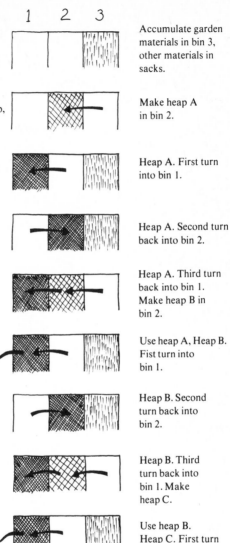

Accumulate garden materials in bin 3, other materials in sacks.

Make heap A in bin 2.

Heap A. First turn into bin 1.

Heap A. Second turn back into bin 2.

Heap A. Third turn back into bin 1. Make heap B in bin 2.

Use heap A, Heap B. Fist turn into bin 1.

Heap B. Second turn back into bin 2.

Heap B. Third turn back into bin 1. Make heap C.

Use heap B. Heap C. First turn into bin 1.

and so on.

SCHEME FOR FULLY AEROBIC HEAP

Activators

Compost activators fall into two main classes: material containing a high proportion of nitrogen, and products whose mode of action is a little obscure but which appear to work as bacterial stimulators or inocula.

The need for the first has already been made clear. The optimum conditions for aerobic bacteria require a mixture of materials in which the proportion of carbon to nitrogen (the C/N ratio) is about 30:1. But the C/N ratio of most garden weeds averages 60-70:1 and to bring this closer to the required ratio we must add materials with a much lower C/N ratio, in other words with a much higher proportion of nitrogen. As such materials are rather hard to come by they have been put in a special category and called activators.

Natural activators are manure, especially chicken manure, urine, pomace (cider residue), hops, comfrey, or any of the materials in the list on page 14 with two or more crosses under nitrogen. Chemical activators are sulphate of ammonia, or any of the nitrogenous fertilizers. Most of the proprietary activators you buy in shops consist principally of chemical nitrogen fertilizer in one form or another. Generally speaking activators of this type do not have any advantage over an ordinary chemical nitrogen fertilizer and the decision which to buy is a matter of comparing costs.

The convinced organic gardener will not use a chemical activator, but many uncommitted people argue that it is better to have a chemical activator than no activator at all. This is a debatable point and I do not think that at present there is any convincing evidence comparing the quality of compost made with organic activators against that made with chemical activators.

A Natural Activator

For some people the issue does not arise because there is one very good organic activator available to everyone who is willing to take a little trouble, and that is what is politely known as *night soil*. Urine is one of the very best sources of organic nitrogen there is, and is freely available to everyone in quantity. The only problem, apart from the embarrassment that some people experience in the operation, is how to apply it without waterlogging your heap.

The best method is to have a large plastic bin, in which you place a layer of dry soil, peat, sawdust or other dry material (not newspaper). Add the daily dose of urine, and continue to add dry material so that it does not become waterlogged. As a second best you can add it to your anaerobic pile of garden weeds, again with an admixture of dry materials, and cover it over tightly with plastic. Inevitably by this method a certain amount will seep away and be lost and the plastic bin method is undoubtedly better. There is no reason why you should not use the same bin as for your kitchen rubbish; make sure though that it has a piece of plastic held down tightly as a seal.

If you use this method you should not need to bother with any other activators, but whatever you do it is important that you are aware of the problem of nitrogen and of the need to take it seriously. Food, water, air, warmth: who can decide which is the most important to life? It is impossible to say since they are all essential. It is more a matter of which of them is in short supply and difficult to obtain. Water is free; air is free but has to be made available by turning; if not its absence will act as a limiting factor. Warmth is taken care of by insulation. Food is the other limiting factor, the necessity to have a balanced diet, and the primary importance of the balance between carbon and nitrogen.

As for the second class of activator, it is very hard to give advice. It has always seemed to me a sort of miracle that this huge and variegated microbial army should assemble and go into action spontaneously and naturally, without any of the elaborate planning that preceded D-Day. The exact details are not known because of the difficulty researchers have had in isolating and studying the individual facets of this multifarious operation. The mere fact of isolating an organism is liable to change its behaviour and even structure in ways that are very hard to determine.

What is evident, though, is that there are very large numbers of different organisms involved in the process and that the ones that prevail depend very much on the particular ingredients of the heap. These emerge in the very rapid 'survival of the fittest' operation which develops, and there is no evidence either theoretical or in practice to suggest that any external stimulus is necessary or beneficial.

What is sometimes claimed is that supplementing the natural population of organisms will enable the whole process to develop more rapidly and efficiently; the suggestion being that there is an initial time-lag, during which the bacteria sort themselves out, which can be eliminated by providing the right organisms with some sort of boost. But several studies (notably at the University of California, for many years the main centre for research into composting) have failed to establish that such a time lag exists. All the evidence seems to confirm that if the right conditions are present decomposition will take place without external aid, and that if the right conditions are absent no amount of activators of this sort will make good the deficiency.

However, it must be conceded that many observant gardeners have used one or other of these activators for years and are convinced of their benefit. At no stage is scientific research infallible and there is still a vast amount to be learnt about how compost heaps work and how best to make them. I would suggest that as an insurance that is both trouble-free and cost-free it is a good idea to incorporate a proportion of compost from previous heaps into the new heap, say about ten per cent, which works out at about twenty good spadefuls for an average-sized heap, spread as evenly as possible throughout the centre of the new heap. It has already been suggested that the partially composted front and top of the old heap should be carried forward to the new one, and this I think should serve the purpose.

Manure

Manure, having a comparatively high nitrogen content, is the commonest activator of the first sort (that is, the sort that provides nitrogen) and probably the best. It must however be fresh, as 'well-rotted' manure will already have been digested by bacteria and become composted, and will have lost its value as an activator. To keep manure in a fresh condition so that it may be used over the season, and also to prevent it smelling and causing a nuisance to over-sensitive neighbours, it must be tightly sealed in bags or kept tightly under a plastic sheet. This will slow down decomposition to a minimum and prevent loss of nitrogen. Manure is usually bought mixed with straw. There should not be too much straw or all its value as an activator will be used up in decomposing the straw and there will be no surplus for your needs.

An undue excess of straw will always retard a compost heap because of its very high cellulose content and the difficulty of breaking it down. On the other hand, if there is a shortage of straw, manure is rather difficult to handle as it forms into sizeable lumps that are completely anaerobic and will take a very long time to break down. In this case, it needs to be thoroughly forked and fluffed around so that it does not lie in heavy wet lumps.

The above remarks apply only to manure as an activator. Of course if you lay in a load of manure for use direct on the garden it may be 'well-rotted' as this will save you the trouble of composting it yourself.

Lime

It is not normally necessary or especially desirable to add lime to a compost heap at any stage. If you live in an area of acute acidity and feel that there is need for some neutralizer, the use of calcified seaweed is preferable to lime.

It is, however, a good idea to measure the acidity of your finished product, and very simple kits are now available for doing this. Acidity is measured by a number, known as the p/h value, which will usually lie between 5 and 8.

Most plants grow best in a soil with a p/h of between 6.4 and 6.8, and if your compost has a value very much below this it is advisable to apply a sufficient quantity of lime or calcified seaweed to bring the p/h up to 6.5. This is likely to happen if decomposition has been mainly anaerobic, and it can serve as an indication that for best results an aerobic heap should be aimed at next time. Lime should not be applied to fresh manure as this will lead to a loss of nitrogen in the form of ammonia. The same will apply to a compost heap before it has decomposed unless you know from experience that it is excessively acid. In a normal aerobic heap the acidity will vary somewhat throughout the cycle, but will end up about correct, that is, at about 6.5.

Woodash

Woodash is valuable because it is a source of potash, one of the principal nutrients required by growing plants. It is often applied directly where it is known to be especially valuable, for instance to beans, potatoes, tomatoes and gooseberries. Otherwise it is better to incorporate it into the compost heap rather than apply it directly. The reason for this is that woodash, although usually designated an organic fertilizer, is not organic in the sense that, say, bonemeal is organic, because it has been reduced to a mineral form by burning. The potash is in a fairly concentrated chemical form that can cause scorching, and is also highly water-soluble, so that a good downpour of rain can wash it right through a light soil. In the compost heap it will be converted to organic forms that are more stable and will not leach away.

As already mentioned woodash is also valuable when the compost ingredients have become too wet. If this is liable to be a problem for you, you should collect it when it is dry and store it in waterproof sacks until the need for it arises.

Potash shortage is sometimes serious in areas with very light soils where the tendency for it to become water-soluble causes it to leach away very easily.

Granite Dust

Granite dust is sometimes recommended, especially in America, either as an additive to the compost heap or as an organic fertilizer or leaf spray. Its exact function or value has not been clearly explained, but it possibly results from the fact that some granites contain a proportion of potash-felspar which could become converted in the compost heap by either microbal or chemical action into forms which make it available as a plant food.

A form of granite dust, also known as dolomite, contains magnesium which is, after nitrogen, potash and phosphate, an essential ingredient of plant food. For this reason dolomite is an accepted fertilizer which is approved of by organic purists.

Phosphate

As well as nitrogen and potash, and to a much lesser extent magnesium, phosphate is the other principal nutrient required by plants. It is not often in short supply but bad soil conditions, especially too acid a soil, can lock it up and make it unavailable. However, if you employ some of the green manuring techniques mentioned later some extra phosphate may be advisable. This will be dealt with in the chapter on green manure. A similar technique can be used for phosphate as was suggested for potash, that is, a chemical fertilizer such as superphosphate can be added to the compost heap which will turn it into an organic form which will become available slowly as it is needed. This would definitely not be approved of by the dedicated organic grower and unless you have good reason to believe that your soil has a serious long-term phosphate deficiency it is not a course to be recommended.

Animal-Free Compost

There are a number of people who on ethical, religious or horticultural grounds prefer to use an animal-free compost. It is worth pointing out two things: one is that the natural process upon which compost-making is based involves a variable mixture of both animal and vegetable matter; the second is that no compost is strictly speaking animal-free since every ounce of it contains many millions of bacteria, to say nothing of the detritus of larger animals, worm-casts, bird droppings, etc. However, these are not conclusive arguments against this point of view, and the whole question of animal-free organic fertilizers is one which demands the attention of those who wish to increase our area of arable land at the expense of mixed farming, and who are also opposed to chemical fertilizers.

For the garden composter, an animal-free compost poses a serious problem of how to provide an adequate supply of nitrogen, because although such sources as hop manure, pomace and seaweed do exist they are not readily available or cheap. Grass mowings and other greenery contain a fair percentage of nitrogen but as this is usually calculated on a dry weight basis and as green plants are roughly ninety per cent water this does not amount to much in practice.

The best plan would be to devote a small area of the garden to a permanent patch of comfrey, and to grow as many legumes as possible, peas, beans, lupins, etc., as these have the ability to fix nitrogen from the atmosphere and are consequently far the best nitrogenous source amongst common garden plants; and in addition to adopt a fairly ambitious scheme of green-manuring: this will be dealt with in chapter 4.

Drainage

If the end product of all your labours is wet and sticky and has a sickly brackish odour of putrefaction, one possible cause is inadequate drainage, a common source of bad composting. It may be that you have positioned your heap in a bad place and nothing can be done about it except to move it. Usually however matters can be improved by raising the heap above ground level. This can be done by leaving the bottom six inches of compost, though of course if this is also wet and sticky, as it almost certainly will be, it cannot be left in this state. This is an occasion when sawdust can be used. The compost should be forked fairly deeply, a large quantity of dry sawdust mixed and turned with it and the whole stamped down again. An inch layer of sawdust can then be spread on top before beginning the new heap, partly to act as a damp-course and partly as a warning against going too deep when you are taking out the compost.

Leaves

Small quantities of leaves may be used in the heap, but should be mixed in with the other ingredients rather than spread together in layers. If you can get hold of large quantities of leaves these should be made into a separate heap. However, this is not quite so straightforward an operation as it sounds as they tend to take up an enormous amount of room and to blow all over the place and you find you need four arms each four feet long – it is rather the same sort of problem as stowing a spinnaker in a force eight gale.

Leaves can be contained in the following way: take a length of 4 ft (1.25m), 2 in (5cm) wire netting and build a fence by weaving 5 ft (1.5m) stakes through the mesh and knocking them a foot into the ground in such a way as to create a container 4 ft (1.25m) wide: you will need 20 ft (6m) of wire netting for a 6 by 4 ft (1.75 by 1.25m) heap and 24 ft (7.25m) for an 8 by 4 ft (2.5 by 1.25m) heap. Pile your leaves into this container, watering them if they are dry (you will need a large quantity of water) and then stamp them down. When this is done, lay a 4 ft (1.25m) length of netting along the top and hold it down with stones.

After a year the heap will have partially decayed and formed itself into hard dense layers, and it should be removed by the same guillotine process as described for the compost heap. It can then be used direct on the soil in

appropriate places, or incorporated into the next compost heap where it will
have much the same beneficial effect as the addition of peat.

On its own leaf mould is excellent for putting into the seed bed, since it

this bit of netting
goes on top to
hold the leaves
and is held down
by bricks

leaves

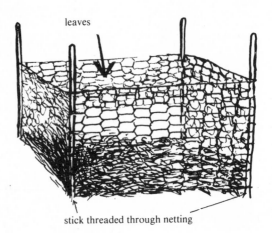

stick threaded through netting

increases the humus content and hence the quality of the soil without unduly
increasing the nutrient content. It also tends to be rather acid, so it is useful
for correcting a soil that is over alkaline, but this has to be watched in a soil
that already tends to acidity.

Leafmould can be such a valuable free bonus for your garden that it is worth going to a little trouble to collect some of the thousands of tons that are wasted every year. This is where a few of those very large plastic bags from electricity showrooms would come in useful.

Straw Bales

One system sometimes advocated is to build the sides of the compost bin with straw bales which after one or two seasons are incorporated into the compost and replaced by further bales. This is an attractive idea for country dwellers with large gardens and large compost heaps. Two cautions need to be uttered: one is that the bales are likely to contain a wealth of weed seeds some of which will certainly spread into the compost. The second is that when they do come to decompose they will need the addition of a very large quantity of nitrogenous matter because of their high ratio of carbon to nitrogen. There is also a danger that selective weed killers were used when the straw was grown. Some of these can remain in the plant for a considerable time and continue to be effective. Many glasshouse crops were lost from this cause when the system of growing on straw bales became popular about fifteen years ago. Ideally therefore only straw grown without weed killer should be used. Unfortunately our planet is now so contaminated by pollutants of all kinds, insecticides, herbicides, radio-active waste, chemical over-fertilization, lead from petrol fumes, industrial pollution, to mention but a few, that attempts to create a healthy soil are almost as problematical as attempts to maintain a healthy atmosphere.

Rough Heap

At various times it has been suggested that such things as brassica stalks, some perennial weeds or wiry grass, should not be put on your compost heap, and it is worth considering for a moment what can be done with these. The simplest answer is to burn them and add the ash to the heap. On the other hand compost, like human beings, benefits from a certain amount of roughage, and there may be a danger that our compost lacks this constituent.

Brassica stalks being mostly cellulose, may be of uncertain value, but there is no doubt about the richness in a dandelion root or a dock; they have delved deep into the earth in search of sustenance and as a result are a mine of mineral wealth. If there is a spell of fine weather and you have the space there is something to be said for spreading the roots out to wilt and dry but this is unlikley to guarantee that they will not grow again; it takes a great deal of drying to sterilize the roots of some persistent perennials. A better plan is to compost them, once again laying them fore and aft so that they can be sliced into small sections, ready to incorporate later into your fast heaps.

This rough heap will of course decompose anaerobically, so perennial roots will not be destroyed. However, it is surprising how much it does break down, provided you keep the weeds cut down and prevented from growing all over the place.

This rough heap is an annual affair, in fact it can easily be left to run on for two years, so it needs to be considerably larger than your normal heaps; being anaerobic it is not essential that it is boxed in, provided you take care not to allow it to spread everywhere.

When you do decide to use it, wait for an opportunity when you have a good supply of fresh manure or other activator. Then guillotine it down as described on page 32 and place it carefully away from the edges of your aerobic heap.

Soil

It is often recommended that soil should be added to the compost heap. Generally speaking there is enough soil in the roots of garden weeds, and in many cases too much. Soil is not necessary in a compost heap, as the example of a manure heap, consisting only of dung and straw, demonstrates. Excessive soil acts as a damper, just as it does in a house fire, or as graphite does in a nuclear reactor. When it can be useful, again as in a bonfire, is as an outer casing to act as an insulator. A three inch layer of soil, or of inverted turves, laid neatly on the top of a completed heap, will have this effect. Soil can be used to a much larger extent in an anaerobic heap, for example, of inverted turves.

Failures

Suppose you have done the very best you can, read all the books, understood them, followed all the instructions, and still your heap produces only a black slimy mess, or a tangle of uncomposted roots?

The main causes of failure have already been mentioned, but here is a summary of them:
1. Too wet or too dry. Is your heap properly protected from the weather? Is it waterlogged from below?
2. Wrong admixture, especially no activator and therefore not enough nitrogen. Also too much hard or woody material.
3. Too much soil, especially perhaps too much heavy clay.
4. Loss of heat. Bin made of corrugated iron, or with big gaps.

5. Material not chopped up properly and/or not mixed up properly, for example layers of grass mowings.

The best course for you to take is to remake or turn the heap, making good the defects as you do so in the ways already described.

3
HOW TO USE COMPOST

Before we actually come to use the compost we should take a good look at it and also at the garden soil. The sort of bacterial bonanza already described as taking place in the compost heap is only an intensification of what is happening everywhere. A teaspoonful of ordinary garden soil is said to contain over 1,000,000,000 organisms. These organisms are all beavering away, going through their spiral of conversion and recycling which is effectively never-ending. Whatever the condition of the soil, there are micro-organisms that can adapt to it. Even if the soil is sterilized it will be re-colonized eventually; if it is sprayed with poison new organisms will evolve that are adapted to survival. Such action will of course harm and perhaps even partially destroy it temporarily, but only some major cataclysm – a new ice age or a nuclear explosion – will destroy life altogether for a long period.

The degree of activity will depend, as in the compost heap, upon the conditions – food, water, air, temperature. In an active soil the nutrients (food) will be continually altering their structure and composition as a result of which there will be a steady stream of nutrients changing into forms that are available as plant food. At the same time the bacteria will as far as possible be maintaining their own environment, the soil, in a condition that suits them, that is open, aerobic, damp, warm – the very same conditions that suit plant growth; in fact there is a happy balance between the needs of the plant and the needs of the bacteria.

It is, I think, important to realize that there is no guarantee, or likelihood, that this balance is especially favourable to the human race or indeed that we have any necessary part in it. On the contrary, it seems evident that with our present numbers and mode of life we completely upset the natural cycle of birth and death, growth and decay. It is because of this imbalance that with heavy-handed arrogance we must intrude our own demands and conditions, asserting the right to totally transform the environment to our own advantage.

What we as compost gardeners are attempting to do is to carry out this transformation in a way that does not too brashly offend against the creative balance that exists. The application of compost is designed, quite simply, to improve the conditions in which a wide range of soil bacteria can operate so that both the physical condition of the soil is satisfactory, and a steady supply of nutrients becomes available as plant food as it is needed.

To this end, the first thing to do is to take a criticial look at the compost we have produced. Is it really the black, crumbly, homogeneous, sweet-smelling material we were led to expect? Or is it cold, grey, glue-like, lumpy and full of inexplicable bits of wire and plastic and long gleaming white roots? If so, these objects must of course be picked or forked out. Now, look again: is it shot through with uncomposted fragments, strawy material, roots, and so on?

If the latter, let us consider what will happen when you mix it into the topsoil: the uncomposted straw represents a surplus of undigested carbon, which is one of the basic foods for bacterial growth. The other two critical needs for bacterial growth are oxygen, which will certainly be readily available in the top soil just after it has been disturbed, and nitrogen, which is probably in short supply or else the straw would already have decomposed. So the bacteria with their natural tendency towards maximum growth, will seek for nitrogen in every nook and cranny of their environment. All the nitrogen therefore which would in the natural course of events have been or become available for plants will instead be re-cycled back into bacterial growth. It will remain in the soil, and will eventually reach that stage in the cycle where it again becomes available to plants, but for the moment it will not be because if there is competition between plants and bacteria for scarce resources, the bacteria will win every time; in this event your plants will suffer from 'nitrogen starvation' and will not grow properly but be chlorotic and stunted. If your compost is as described you have two options: either to sieve it carefully, using a one inch mesh sieve, and recompost the residue; or else to put it on in the autumn and use it to grow a green manure crop, so that it is broken down and ready for use in the spring. The first is probably the better alternative in most cases.

Taking a Soil Profile
The next thing to do is to take a look at your soil, and I would recommend that you take a soil profile. To do this it is usually recommended that you dig a hole three feet deep and to do this it is necessary to make the size at the top at least three feet square, so as to enable you to step it down to reach the required depth.

For our purpose a hole 18 inches square at the top and 18 inches deep should be sufficient. One of the downward faces should be sliced clean and even so that it can be examined. In a fairly typical soil the top few inches will be brown and well matted with roots and other fibrous material. Below that will be a layer of between four and eight inches which is also brown and still has a fibrous texture. This is the top soil and is the most important layer from the point of view of plant growth. Below this there will be another layer which is much lighter and which may very well be rather greyish in colour. This is the subsoil. Below this again you may come to a soil which is quite highly coloured, particularly yellow or red or red-brown. This difference in colour between the two layers is caused by the washing down of iron compounds by rain, and suggests that very probably plant foods and lime are being washed down as well.

DIGGING A THREE FOOT SOIL PROFILE

Examining the Top Soil
Now take a further look at the top soil. How deep is it? How dark is it? How much organic matter does it contain? What sort of texture does it have?

What about the subsoil and the parent soil below? Both of these are important partly because they give a clear indication of the basis of the top soil; partly because of their effect on it — for example as regards drainage; and partly of course because plant roots will be growing into them: even many annuals have a very wide and deep root system: the roots of carrots for instance will penetrate seven feet or more. Is it sandy, silty or clayey? Take a small knob of reasonably moist soil and rub it between your fingers. If it feels gritty and does not dirty the fingers, and cannot be moulded into a cohesive ball, then it is a sandy soil. If it is gritty but can be formed into a ball and does dirty the fingers then it is a sandy loam. If it is not gritty, but sticky and becomes polished when you roll it between your fingers, then it is a clay. If it feels smooth and silky but does not become polished, then it is a silt. If it is none of the above, forms into a cohesive ball and dirties the fingers then it is a loam.

For a sandy soil you must pay particular attention to conserving moisture by incorporating rough compost, by mulching, and by disturbing the surface as little as possible. It is also wise to watch carefully the supply of nutrients, for instance a shortage of potash indicated by brown spot on broad beans, or of nitrogen indicated by a stunted growth and pale sickly leaves. It is also very likely to be an acid soil and to need frequent liming (or treatment with calcified seaweed). If it is clay the addition of lime will help to create a surface tilth for sowing. There is usually no serious shortage of humus or nutrients, and composting should aim at creating a more open soil texture and a more workable soil. Deep-rooting green manure plants will be helpful in improving drainage.

Silt is one of the most difficult soils to work and the need to add large amounts of humus makes the composting and green manuring system outlined in the next chapter especially applicable.

Using Your Compost
We will now proceed on the assumption that you have a fair idea of the type and quality of your soil, and that by one means or another you have achieved a reasonable heap of good quality compost, and now the question is how best to use it.

First of all there is no avoiding one indisputable fact: compost is like money, it is far harder to make it than it is to spend it — and there is never enough, not nearly enough. Therefore every bucket of compost must be used with thrift and care. The important underlying principle is that it should be used when and where plants are growing, that is at root level in the vicinity of plants at the time of maximum growth. So do not spread it all over the garden indiscriminately; do not use it as a mulch except in special circumstances, and do not put it on in the autumn to overwinter. Use it as soon as you are able to, and put it where it will have the most immediate effect. There is a myth that whereas chemical fertilizers, being water soluble, very quickly leach out of the soil, organic fertilizers and compost somehow last for ever. This is not exactly true. If compost is put on the soil in the spring its effect will have mainly disappeared by the autumn – not entirely because there will be some residual improvement in the quality of the top soil, but it will not be very noticeable.

The truth is that if compost is spread wholesale over or in the soil where it is not being used fairly immediately its effects will be largely wasted. Similarly if it is heaped up in a pile waiting for the time when it is needed some of its potency and good effect will be lost.

Luckily compost is mainly produced during the warm months from April to September, and this is precisely the time when most plant growth is taking place and therefore when it is most needed. Below is a list of suggestions of where best to use it for different months, though this will of course depend upon the latitude and the weather conditions. An extra cold year in the north of Scotland could be two to three months behind an extra warm one in St Ives.

March/April	Seed bed, new potatoes, early peas, onions.
May	Greenhouse, asparagus mulch, globe artichoke mulch, strawberries, soft fruit, raspberries.
June	Runner beans, maincrop peas.
July	Planting out brassicas, celery, celeriac, leeks.
August	Planting out brassicas.
September	Planting out seakale and spinach beet.
October November	Broad beans, hardy peas.

Plants that must have a rich soil and plenty of compost
Strawberries, raspberries, black currants, broccoli, sprouts, celery, celeriac, runner beans, maincrop peas, asparagus, artichokes, onions.

Plants that will produce a reasonable crop on less good soil
Lettuces, summer turnip, summer beetroot, spinach, swedes, seakale and spinach beet, Jerusalem artichoke, leeks, savoy cabbages, kale, broad beans.

It should be understood that there are very few, if any, vegetables that will not do better on a well-composted soil; the above are ones which will produce some sort of worthwhile crop on soil of only medium quality.

Plants which definitely dislike fresh manure or compost
Carrots, beetroot, spring cabbage (when they are planted out).

With this information it should be fairly easy to know how best to allocate limited supplies of compost, and the following notes mainly amplify the obvious.

For all plants and seeds that are normally trenched, a one or two inch layer of compost is put in the bottom of the trench and the seeds planted in it. When planting leeks or potatoes by the dibber method a small handful of compost is put into each hole, and the plant set on top of it. Salsify and scorzonera should always be sown by making a hole with a crowbar, filling with a mixture of sifted compost and fine soil which is watered and firmly compacted, and sowing two or three seeds in the centre. Long parsnips are best sown that way too if your soil is in the least bit heavy, and even maincrop carrots if you want a good crop.

In poor soil small seeds can be sown as follows: make a small trench about two inches wide and one and a half inches deep. Water thoroughly if the weather is dry; fill with damp compost, tread down firmly and level off with the back of a rake, and sow the seed in this.

When transplanting brassicas or other plants (except spring cabbage) make a larger hole than necessary and plant in compost.

Seed Bed
It is often said you should not put too much compost on your seed bed because this will result in a growth of seedlings that is too rapid and sappy. This might be true if you put on too much very rich compost, but this is not very likely – there is a far greater danger of too little.

The conditions necessary for good seed germination are warmth; air (oxygen); and moisture.

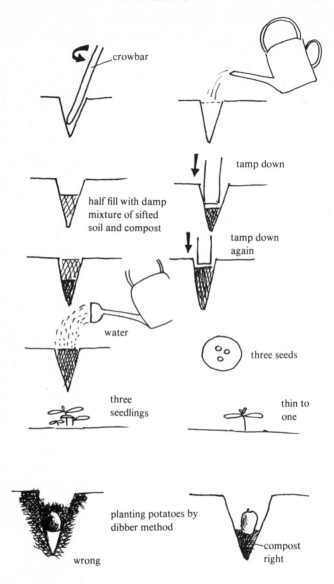

crowbar

half fill with damp
mixture of sifted
soil and compost

tamp down

tamp down
again

water

three seeds

three
seedlings

thin to
one

planting potatoes by
dibber method

wrong

compost
right

The need for oxygen means that the soil must be open, that is it must have a good tilth; the need for moisture means that although open it must not dry out, that is, it must have a good content of organic matter; and the need for warmth requires it to be light in texture and dark in colour.

All this points to a soil with a high proportion of organic matter, and the seed bed is the one place where you must be prepared to spread compost over the whole area. In addition if you have been using peat for storing roots, or for forcing chicory, or for blanching celery, or in potting compost, it is on the seed bed that it should end up. It is difficult to say how much compost you should use, because it rather depends upon how you manage your seed bed in other respects, in particular how much soil you take off on the roots when you are transplanting. In general you should aim to spread at least one inch depth of compost or peat every year, that is, at a rate of about one barrow-load for a bed eight by ten feet (2.5 by 3m).

Planting Fruit Trees, Shrubs etc.

The main aim when planting is to induce a prolific root growth well below the surface so that the plants grow rapidly as soon as the soil warms up in the spring and so that they do not dry out in the warm spells of May and June. Many shrubs (for example raspberries and roses) have a tendency to surface rooting with a consequent danger of drying out during hot spells; it is necessary therefore to maintain a good rooting system well below the surface to guard against this, which is why it is so important to incorporate compost *beneath* the roots at planting time. Trees and shrubs cost quite a lot of money nowadays and will continue to give you service for many years. A little extra care at planting will affect them permanently so it is really worth taking that extra care. The following method should be observed very carefully.

Preparation of the Soil

It is essential that the soil should be very firm at planting time; therefore any preparation should be carried out *at least* four weeks in advance to allow the soil to settle. It is very bad to dig out a lot of deep-rooted perennial weeds one day, and plant trees in the same soil the next. But if this does happen the only thing to do is to ram and stamp the soil down as much as you can. If your soil is too acid, counteract this with calcified seaweed in preference to lime.

Arrival of Plants

If you cannot plant immediately lay them out and cover roots with several layers of damp sacks or damp soil. On no account must the roots be left to dry out. This is very important. If they are container grown, leave them in

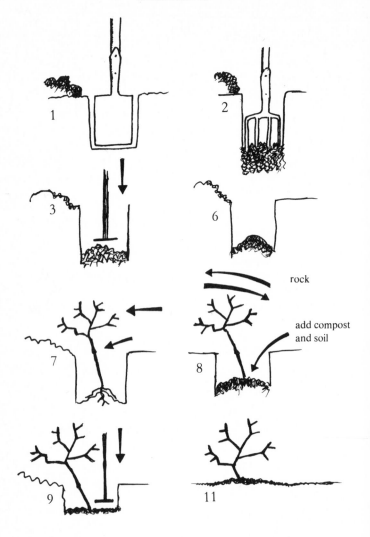

their containers till planting time, placing them in a sheltered position out of wind and sun. Remember to keep them moist by watering.

Preparing for Planting

Trim roots (in the case of young shrubs to about twelve inches long), removing any that are damaged. Shorten top growth. Mark the bed with sticks to make quite sure where you want to plant.

Planting

You will need a one-gallon bucket of water per plant (two if the weather or soil are dry) and a bucket of compost, (two if the soil is poor). If you have any wool shoddy, horse hair or bristle, this is a very good place to use it for it will continue to decompose, slowly releasing nitrogen over several years. It is very important that it is thoroughly wetted, especially in the case of shoddy.

1. Dig hole one full spit deep with spade. Put the top soil on one side and the sub-soil in a barrow to take away.
2. Loosen soil for another spit with fork.
3. Incorporate half your compost into the second spit, mixing it with the soil. Ram this mixture down *very firmly*.
4. Mix the other half of the compost with the top soil from the hole.
5. Pour on half the water.
6. Make a conical mound at the correct depth (this is unnecessary if plants are container grown.) Unless otherwise instructed this should be at the same depth as the plant was grown in the nursery, indicated by the soil mark around the stem.
7. Place tree or shrub on mound, spreading roots neatly all round it. If it is a windy site lean the plant slightly *away* from the wind. If the plant is container grown make sure it has been thoroughly watered before planting so that when the container is removed the soil or compost will remain attached to the roots, and place it in the centre of the hole. (Note that occasionally containers may consist of peat pots which should not be removed but should be *thoroughly* soaked in water.)
8. Add about six inches of soil/compost mixture. Rock the plant gently back and forth so that the soil gets right round the hair roots, using your fingers to push it through the roots. Once again ram the soil down firmly.
9. Go on adding the soil/compost mixture firming as you go, to about one inch from the top.
10. Pour on the other half of the water.
11. Spread the remainder of the compost/soil mixture loosely on the surface.

For normal soils, the amount of water suggested is the absolute minimum, even in damp conditions or rainy weather. In dry conditions more will be essential. The only possible exception to this is if you live in an area of badly drained heavy clay. This problem is dealt with below.

Firm planting is absolutely essential. It is no good just treading the soil firm at the end as this will leave loose soil underneath just where it matters: the soil must be firmed as you go. If your soil is very clayey and sets like concrete you must add more compost to counteract this but you must still ram it firm.

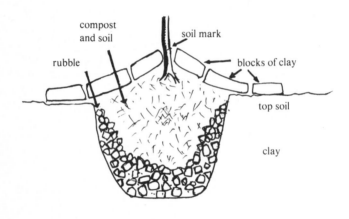

Dealing with Clay

There is one situation where the method described above will not work and that is if your land is a low-lying heavy clay that will not drain, for example much of the Thames Basin. What happens here is simply that the rainwater runs into your nice well-composted, well-drained soil and fills up your hole where it remains indefinitely, waterlogging your plant roots. There is not really much you can do about this, short of digging a simply enormous hole, but even this is likely to fill up eventually during the rainy season. The best thing to do is to dig a large deep hole and stack the clay by the side of it. Fill the bottom and sides of the hole with drainage material, for example mortar rubble, crushed and broken bricks. Plant your tree in a mixture of soil and compost in the normal way, but set the soil mark a little above the level of the soil, building up the compost to this level. Finish off with four inch slabs of clay as shown below.

What you are doing, in effect, is to protect your roots and the soil they are growing in by roofing them in with clay, allowing only a quite small area for the necessary moisture to drain in. All this involves quite a lot of time and trouble, but the only alternatives are to avoid growing trees and shrubs in this sort of area, take a chance that you may lose the plant and your time be wasted, or go to the even greater trouble and expense of installing a system of field drains.

The Fixed Row System

The general guidance given in this chapter should enable any gardener to adapt his gardening practice to compost methods. This book is not intended to be a gardening manual but because the problem so often arises that there is not enough compost to go round I am going to describe now a system of organising the garden that is intended to make the maximum use of what compost there is.

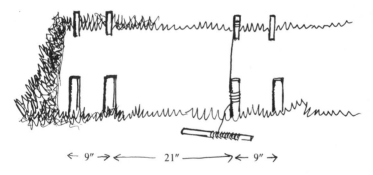

← 9″ → ←——— 21″ ———→ ← 9″ →

The basis of this system is that the same area should be used year after year for growing crops that are heavy feeders and that this area should receive the main bulk of the compost, whereas the intervening areas need not be composted to the same extent or even at all, and will be used for the light feeders. Here, what was said earlier should be repeated: there are very few plants that do not prefer a well composted soil, but there are some which will produce a reasonable or at any rate usable crop in soil of only medium quality, whereas there are others that it is just not worth growing unless you have high quality soil.

The basis of this system is that the garden, or a portion of it, is marked out permanently in strips 9 in. (23cm) wide and 21 in. (58cm) apart. All your compost, or the greater part of it, is applied within the strips, and the great majority of the heavy feeders are grown in double, single or triple rows within the same strips. The intervening 21 in. is used to interplant the light feeders and to grow green manure crops, if you adopt the green manuring procedures outlined in the next chapter. Certain permanent crops of course exist outside this system, for instance asparagus or soft fruit. Others also seem better outside it, for example, Jerusalem artichokes, because of their growing habits. Apart from that it is possible to adopt any distribution of crops or any rotation that suits you.

The first thing to do is to mark out your bed with permanent markers. These should be straight strong stakes about 20 in. long which should be hammered a foot into the ground and should remain there permanently. The bed should be measured out accurately and stakes should be placed at each end of the rows. When you are sowing or planting you should always use a line and this should be wound round or aligned to the stakes. Occasionally the stakes can get loose or get kicked out or broken, and then they should be replaced at once.

A typical rotation over a cycle of three years would be:

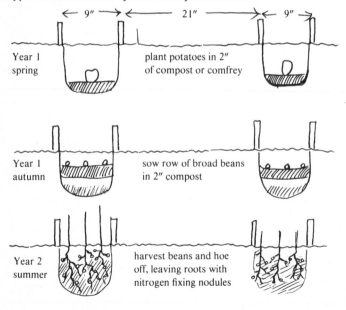

Year 1 spring — plant potatoes in 2" of compost or comfrey

Year 1 autumn — sow row of broad beans in 2" compost

Year 2 summer — harvest beans and hoe off, leaving roots with nitrogen fixing nodules

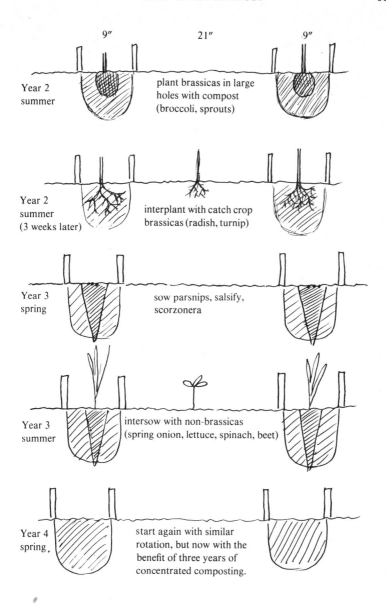

9"   21"   9"

Year 2
summer
plant brassicas in large
holes with compost
(broccoli, sprouts)

Year 2
summer
(3 weeks later)
interplant with catch crop
brassicas (radish, turnip)

Year 3
spring
sow parsnips, salsify,
scorzonera

Year 3
summer
intersow with non-brassicas
(spring onion, lettuce, spinach, beet)

Year 4
spring
start again with similar
rotation, but now with the
benefit of three years of
concentrated composting.

Year 1	_Year 2_	_Year 3_
Spring Plant maincrop potatoes in trenches with 2 in. of compost. _Autumn_ Harvest potatoes and follow with triple row of broad beans in trenches with another inch of compost.	_Summer_ Harvest and hoe off at surface level, leaving roots to rot. 　　　Plant　brassicas, preferably　sprouts　or broccoli　(now　called 'winter　cauliflower')　or sprouting broccoli. _Summer/Autumn_ Inter-plant with crops of brassicas, either transplant kohl rabi, summer cabbage, or sow catch crop of turnips or radish.	_Spring_ Lift brassicas. Level off and plant parsnips, scorzonera, salsify, etc. _Spring/Summer_ Intersow with spring onions, cos lettuce, spinach, beet, carrot.

In the spring of Year 4 start again with a similar rotation, but now with the benefits of three years of concentrated composting.

The advantages of this scheme are obvious, but there are of course some disadvantages, which do not seem to me to amount to very much, but which should I think be mentioned:

1. Adhering to it does require a considerable amount of discipline and planning. The position of the rows must be carefully marked and adhered to. Intercropping must be carefully planned and must take advantage of the period when main crops are not too large or too vulnerable.

2. The distance between rows is geared to the crop requiring the greatest distance, that is $2\frac{1}{2}$ feet. But the fact is that whatever the gardening books may say, the distance between rows is arbitrary anyway and as much determined by convenience and custom as by logic. If some crops are spaced wider than they normally demand this can be made up by planting closer in the rows, and also of course by a greater use of the space between the rows for interplanting.

3. The space between the rows remains barren and of poor quality. This need not be quite true, as will be shown later in the chapter on green manure. My own feeling is that generally speaking the great advantages of building up this concentrated channel of rich composted growing medium for your principal crops far outweighs the minor disadvantages.

A great many variations on this rotation are possible, and a few are shown below:

Crop	Sow/Plant	Harvest
Potato Runner bean Maincrop peas Cauliflower Tomato Onions	Spring/early summer	Autumn
Broad beans Hardy peas Spring cabbage Spring lettuce	Autumn	Early the following summer
Sprouts Broccoli Sprouting broccoli Kale Swede Celery Celeriac Leek Beet	Summer	Up to following spring

This is shown more clearly in the following diagram from which it can be seen that the *sine qua non* of this rotation is the broad bean, for it is the only seed that can be sown late enough in the autumn to follow late summer crops, germinate, grow through the winter, and produce a crop by the end of it. It is a legume, and so it fixes nitrogen, is virtually disease free, and is exceptionally easy to grow. It is true that the hardy pea has similar advantages but it cannot compare with the bean for reliability and usefulness, either as an edible crop or as a producer of green manure. Also, of course, the field, or tic, bean has many similarities to the broad bean, and many similar advantages; its disadvantage is that to produce a crop it has to stay in the ground until very late in the summer and this limits the choice of crops that can follow it.

The above description may give the impression that we are leaving a fair proportion of the garden infertile, but this is not exactly the case. Our aim is eventually to get the whole of it into a highly fertile condition. What we are doing is to ensure that when there is a limited amount of compost available, as tends to be the case, especially in the early stages, then the heavy feeders get priority.

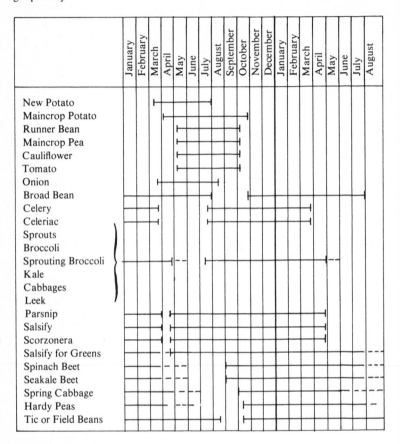

Notice, too, that this rotation is far easier to operate under a no-digging system. Digging is not excluded but care must be taken to maintain the line of the compost rows and retain the compost in them, which is not easy if you dig to any depth. This question of no-digging is examined briefly in chapter 5.

You will realize by now that just as the broad bean occupies a dominant position in your crop rotation, so it will tend under this system to occupy a correspondingly dominant position in your diet. This is accentuated by the fact that it gives not one crop but three. First the tops should be picked off in April or May as soon as three or four trusses of flowers have blossomed; this produces a useful, though unexciting, variation in the diet of greens that are dominant at this season. A few weeks later immature bean pods may be picked off when they are two or three inches long and cooked whole, or chopped up and eaten raw in salad; and lastly the familiar podded bean in late June and July.

4
GREEN MANURE

As has been said already, all life on this planet derives ultimately from the ability of plants to use the energy of the sun to enable them to build up complex organic compounds which then either feed higher organisms or else decompose to create fertile soil. There is a third way in which plants benefit us: by storing the energy of the sun which would otherwise be radiated out into space and wasted. The importance of these three functions calls into question the time-honoured practice of aiming at a weed-free garden, an artificially maintained expanse of bare soil in which rows of selected plants are permitted to grow in glorious isolation, living like monks or kings uncontaminated by the proximity of lesser mortals.

In addition, during the winter, when it is difficult to think of useful crops to grow, the ground is left bare so that frost can act upon it. Both these practices are in opposition to the need to maximize the use of the sun's energy, but this is a question that is very seldom given sufficient or even any consideration in organizing the garden or planning rotations. On a practical level it is an important factor in maintaining the fertility of the small garden, especially when organic material is hard to come by. So long as the soil is left bare its potential value as a converter or storer of the sun's energy is being wasted. As a general rule, therefore, all ground should be fully covered with growth for as much of the time as is practicable in order that the maximum amount of plant growth is achieved and the maximum amount of the sun's energy is used. What is not consumed by animals or humans is then returned to the soil to build up its fertility.

Leaving Fallow
Not many gardeners nowadays would be happy with the 'fallow year' technique where land is deliberately left uncropped to enable it to grow a mixed crop of weeds which are then turned back into the soil. If green manuring is going to be practised then some method of incorporating it into

the general garden routine without sacrificing edible crops must be found. It is comparatively simple to grow a crop of some sort through the winter and this is far better than leaving the ground bare. Exposing the soil to frost, which is the principal reason for leaving the soil bare, is undoubtedly effective and does increase its friability, particularly in the case of clays or silts, but this is only a physical rearrangement of what is already there, which is confined to the top few inches of soil and which effects no permanent improvement to the quality of the soil. The incorporation of organic matter, however, actually changes the soil by altering its components and structure, and so helps to build up its long-term fertility.

The question of growing green manure crops between edible crops is more controversial because it is necessary to be sure that this is not detrimental to the growth of the edible crop. However, as with the fallow year, there is a time-honoured precedent in the undersowing of grain crops with clover and similar practices.

There are two main opportunities for growing green manure crops in this way: the first is to sow catch crops where the land is temporarily vacant between lifting one crop and planting the next, or before a crop has grown to any size. The second is to undersow crops that will be removed and which will then be replaced by the already established green manure.

Fenugreek

For the first, the traditional crop is mustard. This has a disadvantage that it is a brassica and could thus increase the vulnerability to club root. A better choice is fenugreek, which is not so prolific of green growth but which is a legume and thus fixes nitrogen, and which is also edible (at least the Indians think so!) Seed is occasionally obtainable from seed merchants for sprouting, but is much more cheaply bought from Indian shops where it is sold as *mehte* and used as a flavouring for cooking. If used for green manuring it should not be allowed to go to seed, but should be cropped as soon as it begins to flower. In the summer it will produce a useful crop within eight weeks and so it may be used to fill in a gap where there is not sufficient time to grow an edible crop. As well as being sown when land is vacant it can be sown between crops in their early stages because normally the distance between rows is determined by their eventual size or by the needs of access. There is no reason at all, for instance, why the space between peas or beans whose purpose is mainly to allow you to pick them, should not be carpeted with a green manure crop rather than left bare.

Here is a list of some typical uses:

March/April Broadcast on top of Jerusalem artichokes immediately after they are planted at least three inches deep.

April Immediately alongside rows of potatoes: the green manure will eventually be buried when the potatoes are earthed up.

May Between rows of maincrop peas.

June On top of the ridges alongside celery trenches.

July Broadcast over the onion bed and allow to grow until onions are lifted.

At any time between widely spaced rows (of peas and beans, for example) where you are not intending to grow a food crop.

There are occasions when a catch crop of this sort should not be sown: for instance, where it will compete for food or moisture with edible crops; where an edible catch crop might be sown instead, or where a more valuable long-term green manure ought to be sown.

The list above is not comprehensive: anyone who is capable of forward planning, and who bears in mind that bare earth, or ground covered with unproductive weeds, is land that is not being used to its full potential, will be continually finding places that can safely and profitably be sown in this way.

Undersowing or Intersowing

The main use for this is with crops that will be lifted during the winter when it is too late to resow the ground, a technique that is particularly applicable to brassicas (sprouts, broccoli, cauliflowers, cabbages etc). Some time after planting should elapse to allow the brassicas to establish themselves and put out a root system: in reasonable weather (not too hot and dry) a period of about three weeks should be enough. Here is a list of green manure crops that can be used and their sowing times. There are several other green manure crops that could be sown to give variety, but it seems better to not overload people with complicated choices:

Plant main crop	Sow green manure	Green manure crop
Late June to July	Mid-July to early August	Clover (preferably Crimson clover, *trifolium incarnatum*) Melilot (sometimes known as Sweet clover) Lucerne (known as Alfalfa)
August	Late August September	Winter tares Hungarian Rye

If you are using the fixed-row system described in the last chapter, then it will normally be an advantage to wait until the intermediate (summer) crop is lifted before sowing the green manure crop, and to try and make these coincide.

For sowing after September you will have to fall back on the good old broad bean, which quite apart from its edible crop is a serious contender for the green manure championship title. A word of warning is needed here though: it is important to understand that beans sown as green manure are treated as green manure and not clung on to in order to get a crop of beans in July, or the whole cropping routine of your garden will go to ruin. It takes quite a lot of character to ruthlessly lift row upon row of broad bean plants in May knowing that in only a month or two they will be producing a handsome crop; but it must be done.

We are now in a position to reconstruct the rotation shown in the last chapter filling in the contribution that green manuring can make without interfering with the cropping. I should like to emphasize again that this is not a gardening book, and this does not represent a full rotation or even necessarily an ideal one: it merely illustrates the sort of rotation that can be worked out.

How to Use the Crop

We now need to consider what we do with our green manure crop when we have grown it. There are two main choices: either we remove it and use it on the compost heap, or we turn it into the ground where it is. There are two dangers with the latter: one has already been mentioned, that, if the proportion of carbon is too high, there will be a danger of nitrogen starvation. This can be guarded against by using green manure crops with a high nitrogen content, such as legumes, and also by never allowing them to grow to a point where they become woody or seedy. The second danger has yet to be mentioned since it never occurs when applying compost to the garden, but it can do so with green manure, and that is an excess of nitrogen. The effect of this will be again to stimulate very energetic bacterial activity which will use up the carbon in the soil. A proportion of the carbon will be converted to carbon dioxide and taken up into the atmosphere, and this will deplete the organic content and fertility of the soil. This will not immediately affect plant growth but will affect the long-term maintenance of the soil structure.

The fact is that in nature there is a process of growth and decay which is never static but which maintains a reasonably balanced and stable continuity. You are engaged in increasing its efficiency of action, but if you do this

	← 9″ →	← 21″ →	
	Principal Crop	**Intersown Crop**	
		Edible Crop	**Green Manure Crop**
YEAR 1 Spring	Plant maincrop potatoes 5in. deep. Intersow with fenugreek	Early peas	Fenugreek
May			
June		Lift	Hoe off
July		Transplant 2 rows lettuce	
August			
Autumn	Lift potatoes, sow 3 rows broad beans		Sow 4 rows broad beans for green manuring
Winter			
YEAR 2 Spring			Hoe off broad beans leaving roots to rot in the ground
May		Sow turnips, summer cabbage, kohl rabi, radish (brassicas)	
June			
July	Hoe off broad beans		
August	Plant sprouts		Sow crimson clover
Autumn			
Winter			
YEAR 3 Spring	Lift sprouts Sow parsnips, salsify	Sow Summer vegetables (not brassicas)	Hoe off clover as ground is needed
May			
June			
July			
August			
Autumn			
Winter		Transplant winter lettuces, spring cabbage	
YEAR 4 Spring	Lift parsnips Plant maincrop potatoes		

abruptly you are bound to upset the dynamic balance of the soil and this has the danger of disrupting the whole process.

On these grounds I think that generally is is better to decompose green manure crops in the compost heap rather than turn them into the top soil. There are exceptions, though. For instance if you are trying to improve a very heavy soil, one technique is to grow legumes with a considerable root system (clover, lucerne). Hoe them off at ground level and leave the roots to rot in the ground. Legumes have a reasonable balance between nitrogen and carbon, and the roots will rot down *in situ* leaving an intricate network of little channels which will help aeration and drainage and improve the physical condition of the soil.

There is an important distinction between the two methods of using green manure explained above. If you turn green manure into the soil where it was grown you are increasing the fertility of the soil. If you take the crop off to the compost heap you are temporarily reducing the fertility of the soil, and if you then use the compost elsewhere you are permanently doing so. In this case you must be careful to make up for that loss when you are next sowing or planting.

Whilst on the subject of green manure it is worth mentioning a few plants which it is worth growing for their contribution to the compost heap, quite apart from any other value they may have:

Jerusalem artichokes The tops can be cut off in July at about four to five feet to stop them blowing over. The remainder of the stem should be cut in the autumn after it has gone brown and is rather less useful.

Sunflower The whole plant is very good for compost; it is better cut when green. They may be grown very close together in some out-of-the-way patch and will still produce sizeable flowers.

Sweet corn As grown on the farm for silage sweet corn produces up to forty tons per acre between May and August, but this of course depends upon growing plants very close together, though even so it will still produce eatable cobs.

Comfrey Comfrey is probably the most valuable producer of compost material there is, but it does have some disadvantages. It occupies a site permanently; it is very difficult to get rid of; and although it can be eaten in various ways, it is not an edible crop that finds favour with many. It has a carbon/nitrogen ratio as low as 10:1 which means that it can be used as an activator for the compost heap. It also means it can be crushed and laid direct in trenches in place of compost. As it also has a high potash content it is valuable used in this way for crops that need potash such as potatoes, beans, etc. Comfrey should be planted in any damp out-of-the-way part of the garden, but it needs looking after. Nettles or couch grass will smother it, so it must be kept weeded as far as perennials are concerned. It will smother most summer annuals and to aid this it should be planted closer together than is usually advocated — fifteen inches is a good distance. Plants or root cuttings should be planted at any time of the year except mid-winter, but preferably in the spring.

Comfrey likes a deep rich soil and will repay dressings of manure or fertilizer. It is quite a good way of converting raw or even chemical fertilizer into an organic compost.

Nettles make excellent compost. If you wish to get rid of them you cut them three or four times a year and in two years they should die out. If you wish to keep them as a provider of compost material (some people think they are good to eat too) cut them only twice a year.

Bracken can be eliminated in the same way. It is valuable compost material when it is green, with a very high potash content, but of very little value when it has withered in the autumn.

Rough Grass is not very good material to use in quantity in the compost heap; it is very slow to break down and in a compost heap the guillotine process when you are turning is made very difficult. It is best stacked in some out of the way corner on its own and left to rot down anaerobically over a long period.

Weeds

Weeds themselves are of course a green manure and can be used as such. Under natural conditions the mixture of crops will adjust itself to the soil and in some cases will act to rectify the soil's deficiencies, for example, daisies flourish in acid soil and are rich in calcium which, if the plants are allowed to rot down *in situ*, will counteract the acidity. For this reason many people advocate encouraging weeds in certain circumstances, but there are two objections to this; the first is that nature is in no hurry; her time scale is measured in millions of years whereas we think in terms of decades, years, or seasons. The effect of a natural weedcrop in one season could be very small, and which of us is prepared to wait longer?

The second objection is that there is no reason to believe that any habitat under natural conditions will revert to a state that is specially beneficial to the human race or to the crops that we wish to grow or to the methods that we wish to use. Generally speaking, therefore, it is better to aim for a green manure crop that we believe has specially beneficial qualities. There is only one reservation here, and that is that very little study has been made of green manures, and beyond a small amount of rule-of-thumb knowledge, such as the advantages of using legumes, we do not really know what are the best methods. If this country is to become more vegetarian in its diet and in the uses it makes of the land, and if it is to avoid the increasing use of chemical fertilizers, it is a matter of some urgency to carry out research and experiment in this direction.

Poor Soil

Sometimes when a patch of soil is particularly poor it is decided not to crop it for a time, but to concentrate entirely on green manures in order to improve its fertility.

Several different schemes for this are recommended in different books. Which one you practise depends very much on circumstances. It is no good trying to grow a crop like sweet corn, which is a fairly heavy feeder; so the best thing is to grow a catch crop of mustard or fenugreek and turn it into the soil after about six weeks to produce a base for some further crop. If you start late in the season your choice is limited to rye or winter tares but at other times you can choose between lupins for rapid production of bulk, deep-rooting melilor for clay soils, and crimson clover which will produce a huge amount of greenery and a very attractive crop of flowers after fifteen months.

Here is a list of suitable crops for different needs.

Plant	Sow	In ground	Benefits
Lupin	Spring	Two months or longer	Bulky material, excellent for light acid soils
Melilot or Lucerne	Spring or early Autumn	18 months	Deep rooting system for clay soils
Rye	Up to end of September	Until following spring	Fastest growing winter hardy crop
Tares	Up to end of September	Until following spring	Nitrogen fixer
Fenugreek	Any time, but not hardy	10 weeks	Nitrogen fixer
Mustard	Any time, but not hardy	8 weeks	Good for potatoes because it suppresses potato eelworm

5
ODDS AND ENDS

New Soil

I am always sorry for people inheriting new land or a building plot to whom the following advice is given: 'double dig the plot from end to end. Remove all perennial weeds and every scrap of root; remove all stones, bits of metal, plastic, old bricks, broken glass, broken-down concrete mixers; incorporate a barrowload of manure every four yards, etc., etc.' He must feel as daunted as Hercules did when he first heard about the twelve labours.

I think most gardening writers make very heavy weather of this situation, just as they make heavy weather of the problem of weeds. Of course if your garden really is situated on top of builders' rubble or an old rubbish dump you will have a few problems. However, as this is not strictly speaking a compost problem, and as I have never had personal experience of it, I am going to pass that one by and assume that you have soil of some sort that is capable of being worked and of growing plants. Here is a method that will enable you to grow crops quickly, and should considerably cut down the amount of slog involved.

First of all scythe or cut down the grass and weeds to soil level. Then mark out your row and slice off the turf in neat blocks a spade's width right the way down it. You now have bare top soil, very matted and perhaps quite hard and possibly also full of perennial roots. What you do next depends upon the nature of the soil, the nature of the topgrowth and what you are going to grow. If the soil is completely full of perennial roots (couch grass, thistle, ground elder, etc) then you will have to dig a trench about six inches deep, take the soil away and burn it. Once burnt, the soil can be brought back, mixed with compost and replaced, or clean soil with or without compost can be brought in from elsewhere. If you have only just moved in and have no compost, you will have to go out and buy some on this one and (with luck) only occasion. If you have a clay soil you can grow crops which require some feeding provided you can create a reasonable surface tilth to get them started. Runner beans would be a good crop, sown initially in a box or pots and transplanted individually with compost. Or, later in the season, brassicas transplanted similarly. Kale and savoys are two brassicas that are fairly undemanding as regards soil fertility. If the soil is light, or looks very poor, try to incorporate some organic matter and grow a crop which does not require very heavy feeding, for example spinach beet, beet, turnips or swedes. Do not grow potatoes by this method as you will have difficulty with earthing them up.

Making Use of Turf

The turf that you have removed can either be stacked in a turf pile and allowed to rot down anaerobically for at least a year: this is in fact one of the occasions when an anaerobic heap is a better alternative to an aerobic one. Stack the turves neatly, like a stack of bricks, turf side downwards. Leave the top flat and finish it off with a layer of soil in which is sown a green manure crop such as clover.

Alternatively the turves can be laid upside down alongside the original cut so that they cover up the turf between the cut rows. Here again you sprinkle a layer of soil and sow a green manure crop but on this occasion a quick growing one. An excellent programme would be to sow fenugreek, after about two months hoe it off, cover it over with another thin layer of soil and sow mustard. By this process the soil and double layer of turf will have gone a long way towards decomposition during the summer months.

If you are going to operate the 'fixed row' system the distance between the cuts will be twenty-one inches and there will not be enough turves to cover over the whole area; in fact you will barely be able to cover every other row. You will, therefore, be left with an area of grass and weeds between your rows. This is covered with a newspaper mulch and should be laid thickly: a complete newspaper should be folded to the right width and laid with each sheet overlapping the next by a fair margin. Readers of *The Times* and *The Daily Telegraph* have a distinct advantage here; papers without much bulk may have to be doubled. The paper should then be held down by stones. Although to begin with this will not look very elegant, it will in time lose its garish whiteness and blend in. This is an excellent way to deal with very weedy ground; couch grass, buttercup and the like will be largely eliminated. It is also possible to mulch in this way with black plastic, but I have never found it so satisfactory though I am not clear of the reason for this. Black plastic does have one very definite disadvantage and that is its tendency to encourage slugs.

If you are growing a crop like spinach beet which does not take up a lot of room you could also slice off the intermediate row, which would leave you a distance of only six inches between cuts. This of course could be fully covered by the turves you have cut. In this case there will not be room to grow a green manure crop and it's better to put a newspaper mulch over it which can then be turned down over the turf and tucked into the soil. So we have the following possibilities.

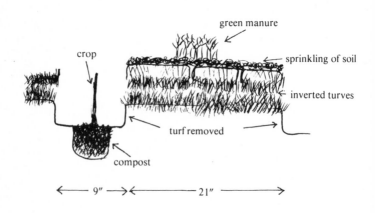

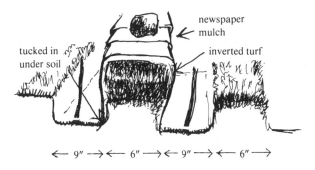

tucked in under soil — newspaper mulch — inverted turf

←— 9″ —→ ←— 6″ —→ ←— 9″ —→ ←— 6″ —→

Of course by this method you are not producing a perfect weed-free crop; grass will sprout out from the edge of your turves. Docks will grow through the top. A whole variety of weeds will surround your crop. Do not worry. About once a fortnight during the growing season just go down the rows keeping things under control. Hoe down the trench. Cut down the sprouting sides with a sickle. Pull off any dock leaves to stop them taking over. If you have some compost by now start to fill up the trenches. Half an hour spent once a fortnight will give you a good start on the long process of getting your garden so that it is not infested with really tiresome weeds. Meanwhile you are growing a crop, you are beginning to make compost, your green manure plants are working on the soil.

It may have occurred to you that the newspaper mulch technique is in total opposition to the idea put forward that the soil should always be growing something, there should never be a bare patch, for nothing could be barer than several thicknesses of *The Sunday Times*. Yes, that is true but the fact is there is no ideal way of gardening, no method that produces the best of all possible worlds in every respect. How you garden is a compromise, or a synthesis if you prefer, of a whole variety of different, and often opposing needs. You should indeed keep your ground growing and working for you as much as you can, but sometimes other needs prevail.

Liquid Manure

In days gone by it was recommended to hang a sack of cow manure in a twenty gallon barrel of water for a month; this produced a thick, scummy liquid which one then diluted down one pint in three, and applied near but not actually on the plants. It is hardly surprising one was advised to keep this dubious concoction away from plant stems and roots, for its strength and maturity were very haphazard and indeed hazardous. Nowadays a similar process is recommended using plants, notably comfrey or nettles or a mixture of the two. Nettles will give a more nitrogenous mixture, and comfrey one richer in potassium. The process is to get a twenty or forty gallon drum, and stuff it with plant material up to a foot from the top. Then fill it up with water (preferably rain water) so that the green material is just covered, and leave it for a month, stirring occasionally, when it can be used undiluted on any of the crops that require feeding.

This can be quite a valuable treatment for plants that require continuous feeding, for example outdoor tomatoes in July and August, celery, marrow, etc. If you are going to apply it in dry weather, it is important to water the plants very thoroughly first. And again, keep it away from actual contact with stems and foliage. It can also be used as a foliar spray if sufficiently diluted, but as the strength of the original liquid is in doubt I do not really advise this unless you are able to carry out trial tests on a small patch first.

Sawdust Toilet

One of the major sources of animal manure is human excreta, but in this country the great majority of this is wasted. One reason often given for this is that it can carry disease. Polio germs for instance will live for two weeks and jaundice can remain infective for considerably longer. But if proper composting methods are used there is no likelihood of any danger. In China human waste is used to produce 200,000,000 tons of compost annually, and I am not aware of any evidence that the Chinese suffer from any diseases or epidemics on account of this.

The following method is described by Hugh Flatt and is reproduced by permission of *Practical Self-Sufficiency* where it first appeared. It is perhaps not a very easy one to practise in an urban or suburban setting, but should present no great problems to the country dweller, except that of getting accustomed to the idea.

'Thirty years ago an elderly woman, who lived in one of our farm cottages, walked three miles every morning during the school term to empty the "earth closet" buckets at the Primary School. One time she was ill for a few days, and as she was a good friend of mine, I offered to do the job to keep it for her. The system, if such it could be called, was a disgrace. The buckets were tipped at random in a corner of a field bordering on the village, where a sloppy, unhygienic, bad-smelling mess resulted. This confirmed my feeling that we should demonstrate a proper, wholesome re-cycling of human waste.

'We have lived on a farm for more than thirty years, where we have had bucket lavatories. We have had a number of visitors during the year, and often two families in the farmhouse; but have not used chemicals. We have used sawdust, or sawdust mixed with soil, in our buckets, adding some each time after use: it is absorbent and sweet-smelling. While it is best to use deciduous sawdust to avoid the resins from the conifers which do not allow it to compost quite so well, I realize this is not always easy to obtain. No disinfectants are ever used.

'A daily routine of emptying the buckets is carried out. The base for the compost heap should be an area of soil (from which worms, bacteria and other soil life can arrive) and it is started with a layer of cut weeds, grass or straw. The contents of the bucket, after tipping are covered adequately each time with such materials as will reduce to a minimum any unpleasant smell, and prevent direct access of flies to the sewage: suitable kitchen waste can be incorporated and from time to time a thin layer of soil spread over (say once in three weeks). If available a layer of farmyard manure can also be incorporated with advantage, but it is by no means essential. The width of the heap should be limited to three or four feet to keep it aerobic, and the length is variable according to space available and the size of heap required before closing; the height of the heap should not be over three to four feet. I have not normally covered these compost heaps, but this could be advisable temporarily during a spell of constant rain which is causing anaerobic conditions. In a prolonged dry spell it can also become necessary to water a heap.

'After three or four months I close the heap and start another: I top up the finished heap with a good layer of green material or straw, finishing with a layer of soil. It is then left for about four months, and then turned once (with a dung fork, moving it all from one end, just shifting it along a couple of feet). This gives it a final aeration and in three weeks or so a fresh-smelling, friable, biologically active compost is ready to spread on the garden: if a heap is not "working" well a little limestone or chalk may help.

'A "Bush Brother" back from Australia told me how, in the British township where he lived, the buckets were emptied at night by the Chinese from a neighbouring township; they never enquired what was done with the material. The British used to purchase vegetables from the Chinese, which they admitted were much better and finer specimens than those they could grow!

'Finally, just because one uses a system regarded as archaic, that is no reason for the "loo" to be dingy, cobwebby and unaesthetic: on the contrary, it is important for it to be bright, regularly whitewashed or decorated. One of ours is out-of-doors and my wife has organised a pleasant approach between flowers and herbs.'

Mulching

Generally speaking mulching has one or more of four purposes: to hold moisture; to suppress weeds; to protect from frost; and to supply nutrients or organic matter to perennial or other permanent plantings.

Mulching can be either localized, where, say, the area in the immediate vicinity of a fruit tree is mulched, or it can be spread over a whole bed. Whatever its purpose it generally has the effect of suppressing weed and other growth as well, so that widespread mulching acts against the precept that as far as practicable the land should be growing a crop of some sort as much of the time as possible. Therefore, although it undoubtedly has its value, widespread mulching does have its dangers.

For example the system of sawdust mulching, proposed by F.L. King, which involves very large areas of the garden being covered by a thick annual mulch of sawdust seems to me to suffer from this disadvantage; this system derives from the example of the forest floor, but in the forest summer sunlight is used to maximum effect by the wide spread of leaves, whereas in a well-mulched garden as much as ninety per cent of the area may be bare soil, or in this case bare sawdust, for much of the summer. Think, for example, of a bed of young sprout plants planted out in July, the regular two and a half to two feet apart.

However, if you can get it, sawdust is a very good mulch for crops like gooseberries and soft fruit generally where the suppression of perennial weeds is important. It will not of course get rid of perennials that are already established, but will act as a deterrent to the growth of new ones.

Here is a list of other occasions when the need for mulching is well established:

Purpose	Plants	When	Material
To conserve moisture and suppress annual weeds	Roses, shrubs, soft fruit, asparagus, globe artichokes	April/May, before the ground dries out	Peat, leafmould, compost, lawn mowings
Suppression of perennial weeds	All types	Anytime	Newspaper, plastic

Purpose	Plants	When	Material
Frost protection	Asparagus, globe artichoke, many shrubs, some flowers (e.g. dahlias)	Autumn	Straw, rough leafmould, bracken, green manure crop
Protecting muddy paths, especially in raised bed growing			Straw, sawdust

Potting Compost

When a commercial grower talks about compost he is referring to potting compost. Just as in this book we have been concerned with using garden compost to improve the soil in which plants can grow to maturity, so potting compost is used to replace the soil in order to grow seeds and seedlings until they are ready for transplanting. Growing seedlings in frames or greenhouses is a more artificial activity than growing plants in the garden; in the garden compost is mixed with soil to produce something that approximates to the sort of natural conditions that plants are accustomed to. In the greenhouse a far more artificial situation exists, when the soil and environment are carefully contrived to ensure maximum germination and survival.

The best seed and potting compost for the organic gardener should be made from the following mixture:

	parts (by volume)
Sifted compost	2
Irish sphagnum peat	2
Horticultural grit	1
Sifted soil	2

This potting compost of course will not be fully sterilized, for quite apart from the sifted soil (which can be omitted) the compost itself is unlikely to be totally sterilized through and through. There is therefore *some* danger of disease, especially of 'damping off' which is a fungus disease transmitted through the soil and which results in small seedlings collapsing overnight. Most large growers sterilize their compost for safety, but small gardeners do not and they usually get away with it. If you do have trouble with this you may have to buy in sterilized potting compost, but I do not know of any such which is fully organic.

Soil Blocks

There is much to be said in favour of soil blocks for use in the greenhouse. They are far cheaper than pots, and more satisfactory than boxes, as each seedling can be planted out without disturbance. It is possible to buy block-making machines, but a very cheap and simple one can be made as follows: buy or acquire (from a dump or building site) a short length of plastic piping of the correct inner width. A three inch pipe is excellent for larger seedlings, a two inch for smaller ones.

Find a bottle that slides easily inside this: an ordinary half-sized wine bottle fits very snugly inside a three inch pipe. You stand the pipe on a smooth surface – a formica top will do very well. Fill the pipe with your compost mixture to the right level for the size of block you require. You will discover what this level is after a very little practice. Ram this down hard with several blows from the bottle. Holding the bottle firmly on top of the block lift the pipe up onto the bottle, using a turning motion, until your block stands free.

An added refinement is to have a screw bottle top or something of that size resting on the formica (possibly fixed on with blue-tak) in the centre of your pipe. This will provide a small indentation in your block for seed sowing. By this method a hundred blocks can be made in a very short time and at the present price of pots this is quite a saving.

Soil blocks should be watered with a fine rose and provided your mixture did not contain too much sand there is no danger of their falling apart. Eventually you will see the growing points of roots emerging from the surface, and this is the time for potting on or planting out.

No-Digging

Compost gardening has come to be associated with the no-digging technique, although of course compost can and should be used to advantage with any system of gardening. I do not really think this book is the right place to try to pronounce judgement on the digging versus no-digging controversy, and in any case I do not feel that there is any cut and dried answer. Generally speaking, I feel that the mistake made by most people is to think that there is just one all-embracing system of gardening that we must follow under all circumstances. Why should this be so? Soils differ; the climate differs; crops

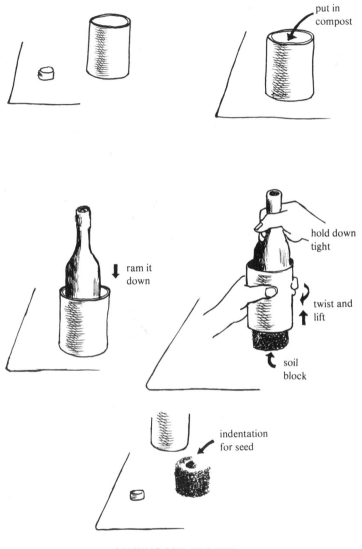

put in compost

ram it down

hold down tight

twist and lift

soil block

indentation for seed

MAKING SOIL BLOCKS

differ, our needs differ; the available technology changes. So also will systems vary to meet these varying circumstances and needs.

On sandy soils there is a need to build up the soil structure by incorporating organic matter. Continual disturbance of the soil would have the following consequences:

Increased aeration

Increased amount of oxygen in the soil

Increased bacterial activity

Increased break-down of complex organic molecules

Increased loss of energy in form of carbon dioxide

An increase of mineralization

A decrease in soil structure

A need for more compost

A decrease in the organic content of the soil

In this case, therefore, the use of a no-digging technique could be generally beneficial in maintaining the organic content and soil structure.

The cycle of events shown above does incidentally demonstrate the fallacy of one widespread argument advanced against no-digging, which is that it requires such gargantuan quantities of compost that it is beyond the reach of ordinary mortals. This is the opposite of the truth. It is the continual disturbance of the soil and particularly of the lower layers that, by increasing the circulation of air, causes the organic matter to be dissipated. From this it is clear that if you have a limited amount of compost available, it is likely to be more economical to use this under a no-digging system than under a digging one.

The case of a pure clay is almost the opposite from that of a sandy soil. Here you are likely to have a soil structure already established: one component of this is a very complex network of cracks which are essential to root-formation. Disturb this and the structure will be broken up, and the soil will become compacted. On the other hand the long-term improvement of a clay soil depends upon the incorporation of organic matter to a considerable depth in order to increase the granulation. So you have a choice, and as with many things in gardening it is difficult to lay down hard-and-fast rules. It is a matter of judgement, but unfortunately in this case there is very little knowledge on which to base this judgement.

What is surprising is that the original inconclusive experiment with comparative areas of digging and no-digging carried out by J.H.L. Chase nearly thirty years ago does not seem to have been repeated or followed up. So we are still lacking really sound practical evidence on which to judge the issue which is clouded with ignorance, fancy, fantasy and prejudice.

Encouraging Worms

One essential for the no-digging technique is to encourage a large and flourishing population of worms who will be the best diggers of all, for they will carry surface organic matter down into the soil, digest it into a form that is suitable for incorporating into the soil, and maintain the soil structure by increasing the granulation.

Essential requirements for the worm are continuous supplies of organic matter, and a soil that is alkaline rather than acid. As plants, generally speaking, prefer a soil that is slightly acid, this means that you must take some care to keep your soil close to its optimum, neither too acid nor too alkaline. A p/h of 6.5 – or just over is the ideal balance, acid enough for plants and alkaline enough for the worms.

Buying In

Ideally the gardener should be able to make enough compost to improve and maintain the fertility of the soil indefinitely and for most soils it should not be necessary to buy any materials in from outside, with the possible exception of lime. However this is an ideal situation which may not be attained for several years; in the meantime compost may have to be supplemented and the question arises what is the 'best buy'.

Manure

You can often buy this in bags at the roadside. If you really have trouble getting your heap to warm up it is worth buying a bag as an activator. For this it must be fresh, it must not have sawdust or chippings; it must not have too much straw; it should not be wet, and it should come from a reliable source; pig or chicken manure from intensive battery units should be avoided. Chicken manure from free range hens is the best of those likely to be available, with a nitrogen content almost twice that of cow or horse manure.

If you are buying manure for use direct on the garden you can either buy it already composted and 'well-rotted', which is simpler, or you can buy it fresh and compost it yourself which is probably better because most farmers are very careless about their manure heaps and allow half the goodness to be wasted.

Peat

Peat is useful for potting compost; for seed beds; for storage of vegetables; for forcing chicory, etc. After such uses it will eventually find its way into the garden. It is inert, contains very little plant food, is usually very acid, and is not a very good buy for direct application to the garden. Particularly uneconomical are very often the 'cheap' bags you can buy at the roadside. Put your hand into these and you will be excited by the damp cool feeling and the peaty aroma. If you take it home and put a handful in a slow oven for a few days you'll wonder what has happened. Where has all that lovely damp peat gone! All you are left with is a tiny little pile of dried-up brown stuff, which is the dry matter content of the handful of peat you put in originally. All the rest of the peat was water and has evaporated!

Here is an analysis of the water content of some typical peats:

	per cent water
Somerset Sedge peat	89.2
Somerset peat (a brand name)	35.05
Irish sphagnum peat	49.3
Cumberland peat	65.6

What this means is that if you buy the Somerset sedge peat you are buying 9/10 water and only 1/10 peat, whereas with sphagnum peat you are buying $\frac{1}{2}$ water and $\frac{1}{2}$ peat. To compare prices therefore the price of the Somerset price must be multiplied by five.

If you have ever had experience of Irish sphagnum peat, you will know that it feels almost bone dry, so it is quite a surprise to learn that it is roughly 50 per cent moisture. Those cool damp dark peats by the roadside often have an even higher water content than the sample I measured, shown above, which was actually a reputable and well-known brand. If you buy peat which has a 95 per cent water content (not uncommon by any means) then you must multiply its cost by 10 to compare it with the cost of sphagnum peat. Once you realize this you see that the roadside peat is not necessarily so great a bargain after all.

Compost

Exactly the same consideration applies of course to buying manure or compost or fertilizer, and it is always worth trying to find out or estimate the water content, so as to get an idea of the true price you are paying. I have seen some 'composted peat' products that were so sticky they must have contained well over 90 per cent water which, according to a quick calculation, would have made the cost around 75p per lb dry weight. The second consideration in buying compost is to make sure it is compost and not a machine dried uncomposted mixture of sawdust and chicken manure from a battery where it may well be contaminated with insecticides that have been used in cleansing the battery house. If you buy mushroom compost make sure whether it was made from horse manure and not from a chemical activator. Also it is wise to test its acidity as many mushroom composts are very alkaline which may be all right if your own soil is acid, but could be harmful if it is not. Many mushroom composts, too, are very strawy and if put on at once will inevitably lead to nitrogen starvation in your plants.

Some composts are 'fortified' with chemical fertilizers, so if you wish to be fully organic these should be avoided.

Sewage Sludge
This is sold by many municipal authorities and is usually in the form of a fine dry powder. It is well-known for producing innumerable tomato seedlings but what seems to be less well-known is the possibility of it containing a dangerous level of some metals such as zinc, lead, etc. Research into this has been carried out under the auspices of the Soil Association and the results are expected to be published fairly soon. In the meantime the use of sewage sludge, particularly in urban or industrial areas, on edible crops is not to be recommended.

CONCLUSION

Throughout this book I have frequently made such remarks as 'although you may use a chemical, the convinced organic gardener would not do so.' How important is it that the compost gardener should be wholly and unequivocally organic? I do not think this question can at this stage be answered on a practical level or from experience; there just is not enough information or knowledge available. For that reason I do not recommend the use of either chemical fertilizers or pesticides if it can possibly be avoided. I do not think half enough is yet known of their ultimate effects on the soil or on our health. Man can hit the moon, split the atom, and blow the whole world to smithereens. He still has not begun to understand the forces at work in a teaspoonful of soil, and the ecology of a cubic yard of hedgerow is too complex for him.

These natural processes, which have taken millions of years to evolve, are affronted by mankind's arrogant belief that we can mould the whole universe to serve our own purposes. Within the brief space of our history we have already overreached ourselves a hundred times. Civilizations have fallen in ruins, the great cities of Ur and Babylon lie buried in the sands, the deserts creep relentlessly on. The bodies of every one of us contain increasing quantities of some of the deadliest poisons ever known. The peregrine falcon is almost extinct in these islands.

I am not suggesting that a packet of metaldehyde or a few ounces of nitro-chalk are responsible for such dramatic disasters. But the acceptance of the doctrine that success lies with combating natural processes rather than co-operating with them contains dangers which are impossible to foresee; and the day of reckoning may be closer than we think.

USEFUL INFORMATION

Organizations

COMET – Combined Organic Movement for Education and Training
Lower Shaw Farmhouse, Shaw, Swindon, Wiltshire

A co-operative effort by all the main organic movements to set up a wider range of courses in organic food production.

No membership
Newsletter: occasional and obtainable free for sae from above address.

HENRY DOUBLEDAY RESEARCH ASSOCIATION
Convent Lane, Bocking, Braintree, Essex

The largest organic organization in the world. Provides a wide and invaluable range of services for the organic gardener, including advice service, green manure seeds and other provisions, seed-finding service and numerous booklets. A must for all serious organic gardeners.

Subscription: £5 a year
Newsletter: Quarterly

FRIENDS OF THE EARTH
9 Poland Street, London W1

A widespread national and local pressure group, much concerned with the provision of allotments and garden sharing schemes.

GOOD GARDENERS ASSOCIATION
Arkley Manor, Barnet, Herts.

Associated with the Horticultural Training College. A much smaller organization than HDRA and The Soil Association, mainly aimed at home gardeners. The Training College is the only one at present offering long-term organic courses for which government grants are available.

Subscription: £4 a year
Newsletter: Eight a year

THE SOIL ASSOCIATION
Walnut Tree Manor, Haughley, Stowmarket, Suffolk

Originally mainly concerned with farming, and now very much directed towards smallholders, training workers, etc. Has a number of local groups throughout the U.K.

Subscription: £5 a year
Newsletter: Quarterly

WWOOF – Working Weekends on Organic Farms
19 Bradford Road, Lewes, Sussex

Organizes weekend and longer stays on organic holdings for its members. Not a training organization, but this is an excellent *entrée* for beginners and can also provide a good introduction to the world of rural alternatives.

Subscription: £2 a year
Newsletter: Every other month

Suppliers
CHASE COMPOST SEEDS
Benhall, Saxmundham, Suffolk

Green Manure seeds

HENRY DOUBLEDAY RESEARCH ASSOCIATION
Convent Lane, Bocking, Braintree, Essex

Green manure seeds
Organic fertilizers
Comfrey plants, and many other items for the garden

ORGANIC FARMERS AND GROWERS
Longridge, Creetings Road, Stowmarket, Suffolk

Organic fertilizers

SELF-SUFFICIENCY AND SMALLHOLDING SUPPLIES
Priory Road, Wells, Somerset

Everything for the smallholder and gardener (Mail Order catalogue 40p)

Further Reading
All Lawrence D. Hills' books are classics. The best buy is the Penguin *Organic Gardening*.

Dr Shewell-Cooper's books cover a vast range, and the best buy is the Faber paperback *The Complete Vegetable Grower*.

A very cheap, very simple, straightforward book for the beginner is *Vegetable Plotter* by Dr D.G. Hessayon. It gives a great deal of information very clearly and, although not organic, its methods can easily be adapted.

Practical Self-Sufficiency (Broad Leys Publishing Co., Widdington, Saffron Walden, Essex). Every other month 60p.

Rural Resettlement Handbook, from Lower Shaw Farmhouse, Shaw, Swindon, Wiltshire. 80p plus 10 in. x 7 in. sae.

Undercurrents (12 South Street, Uley, Dursley, Glos.) Every other month 45p.

INDEX